THE HISTORY OF CODES AND CIPHERS
IN THE UNITED STATES DURING
THE PERIOD BETWEEN THE WORLD WARS
PART II. 1930-1939

Edited

by

Wayne G. Barker

ISBN: 0–89412–165–0 (soft cover)
ISBN: 0–89412–166–9 (library bound)

AEGEAN PARK PRESS
P.O. Box 2837
Laguna Hills, California   92654
(714) 586-8811

Manufactured in the United States of America

FOREWORD

The Historical Section of the Army Security Agency, Washington, D.C. prepared in 1946 a history of codes and ciphers in the United States between the years 1776 and 1939. A "sanitized" version of the history, with classified portions deleted, was later placed in the National Archives as document SRH-001. The original titles of the history were:

Historical Background of the Signal Security Agency —
Volume I — Codes and Ciphers Prior to World War I (1776–1917)
Volume II — Codes and Ciphers during World War I (1917–1919)
Volume III — Codes and Ciphers during the Peace (1919–1939)

In 1978, Volume I, after being edited, was published by AEGEAN PARK PRESS as Volume 20 in its Cryptographic Series, with the title *The History of Codes and Ciphers in the United States Prior to World War I.*

In 1979, Volume II, after being edited, was published by AEGEAN PARK PRESS as Volume 21 in its Cryptographic Series, with the title *The History of Codes and Ciphers in the United States during World War I.*

In 1979, the first half of Volume III, after being edited, was published by AEGEAN PARK PRESS as Volume 22 in its Cryptographic Series, with the title *The History of Codes and Ciphers in the United States between the World Wars, Part I. 1919–1929.*

The present book, *The History of Codes and Ciphers in the United States between the World Wars, Part II. 1930–1939*, which is Volume 54 in the Cryptographic Series of AEGEAN PARK PRESS, completes publication, after editing, of all three original volumes contained in SRH-001.

As in the case of the three previously published volumes, the reader should understand that the present book is not an exact copy of the manuscript as released to the National Archives. In order to make the text readable and to insure continuity in the text, the editor has at times rearranged the text, occasionally adding sentences where deleted portions appear in the released "sanitized" version. The editor, however, hastens to assure the reader that great care has been taken to make the text as historically accurate as possible. Where on occasion the editor has deemed it appropriate to make a comment about some statement of fact or information found in the text, his comments have always been provided as clearly identified footnotes.

With respect to the important decade 1930–1939, when the art of cryptography and cryptanalysis developed into the science of *cryptology,* the editor strongly feels that he should especially pay tribute to William F. Friedman. Not only are Friedman's writings considered today as classic works of cryptographic and cryptanalytic literature, but his keen and astute wisdom was evident in the selection of the particular individuals chosen to be his principal assistants, Solomon Kullback, Frank B. Rowlett, and Abraham Sinkov. Reflecting the dedication and brilliance of their mentor and teacher, the magnitude of the contributions that these persons made to their country during the decade of the 1930's and during World War II can never be really adequately expressed. Not only did these individuals lay the foundation for successful efforts of the United States to break and read the most sensitive messages of the enemy, but through their efforts the secret communications of the United States remained secure during the War. The nation owes an immense debt of gratitude to William F. Friedman, Solomon Kullback, Frank B. Rowlett, and Abraham Sinkov.

October 1989   WGB

ILLUSTRATIONS

CONTENTS

CHAPTER I

FORMATION OF THE
SIGNAL INTELLIGENCE SERVICE

STEPS TOWARD THE ESTABLISHMENT
OF UNIFIED RESPONSIBILITY

The primary result of the investigation conducted by Major O.S. Albright for the Military Intelligence Division,[1] though it was not at once fully achieved,[2] was the unification[3] of responsibility for all cryptological work carried on by the Army in a single organization. It was especially fortunate that this movement toward unification of cryptological responsibilities began when it did, for in the same year (1929) the United States faced the most severe economic depression it had ever experienced. Funds for military purposes, though by no means abundant in the first decade of the Peace, were much more restricted in the second. At a time when Government revenues fell off, it was inevitable that such money as was available should be spent for more pressing needs than that of preparing for a war which to most people then seemed remote, if not impossible. The unification of responsibility made it possible for those concerned with cryptology to present a single request for funds, with the result that a proper balance could be maintained between cryptographic and cryptanalytic activities.[4] Had the diversity of responsibility continued longer, it is doubtful whether sufficient funds could have been obtained to adequately carry on the growing cryptological functions which the Army faced.

---

1. For the story of Major O.S. Albright's investigation, see *The History of Codes and Ciphers in the United States During the Period Between the World Wars, Part I. 1919-1929,* pp. 127-130.

2. Not until 1934 was responsibility for printing, storage, and issue of cryptographic systems assigned to the Chief Signal Officer.

3. A step in this direction had been taken during World War I when the Military Intelligence Division assumed some of the cryptological functions formerly carried on by the Signal Corps, but even then the unification was by no means complete. See *The History of Codes and Ciphers in the United States During World War I,* particularly Chapter I.

    EDITOR'S NOTE: In 1917 the Military Intelligence Division established the Cipher Bureau whose primary function was cryptanalysis; but during World War I, though the Signal Corps did not relinquish its responsibility for the compilation of codes and ciphers, in the United States the Cipher Bureau performed almost all code compilation work for the Army. In France, however, code compilation for the AEF was performed by the Signal Corps. WGB

4. Although the duties of the Signal Corps previously were limited to code and cipher compilation, its responsibilities now included cryptanalytic activities. WGB

That the responsibility should be unified in the interests of efficiency was a fact that does not appear to have needed much discussion. The experience of the preceding decade when no such unity had existed convinced all concerned of the need for a reorganization in this direction. The factors which ultimately justified the placing of a unified cryptological responsibility within the Signal Corps were:

a. The Signal Corps had already established a code compilation section which had done satisfactory work.

b. The chief of this section was a competent and qualified cryptanalyst.[5]

c. He had already participated in training programs, was the author of training pamphlets, was an instructor at Army camps, and was a participant in maneuvers.

d. The Signal Corps was better equipped to develop necessary intercept facilities than any other Army organization; in fact, it was the only such Army organization.

e. The Signal Corps could develop secret ink facilities as well as any other organization.

f. The Military Intelligence Division had no training program; in fact, it had borrowed the services of the Signal Corps cryptanalyst[6] for such limited training exercises as had been possible.

g. The Military Intelligence Division had lost the financial support formerly received from the State Department.

h. Internal difficulties within the Cipher Bureau made a radical reorganization imperative.[7]

i. It was believed desirable to remove the operation of solution and detection services from the General Staff and to place it within an existing operating branch.[8]

---

5. William F. Friedman. WGB

6. In the decade that followed World War I, the Cipher Bureau, under the leadership of Herbert O. Yardley, with much success carried out cryptanalytic tasks for the Army and State Department. At the same time, William F. Friedman, here termed the Signal Corps cryptanalyst, compiled codes for the Army, prepared texts and instructional materials for cryptographic and cryptanalytic training, and periodically gave instruction concerning codes and ciphers at the Signal School. WGB

7. As far as Yardley was concerned there were no internal problems or difficulties in the Cipher Bureau. His biggest problem was lack of traffic. WGB

8. See Memorandum for Colonel (S.H.) Ford from Lieutenant Colonel W.K. Wilson, 18 March 1929; Memorandum for the Chief of Staff from the Assistant Chief of Staff, G-2, Subject: *Responsibility for the Solution of Intercepted Enemy Secret Communications in War* (no date, approved 5 April 1929), sec. 2, par. 3.

Accordingly, it appeared logical "that the Signal Corps should be charged with *all* phases of this work" to the end that it might "be properly coordinated as an organized entity, and still remain as at present under the General Staff control and supervision of G-2."[9] Such a concentration of the entire responsibility in the Signal Corps would eradicate, it was believed, the existing difficulties. Training could be coordinated through the assignment of personnel for technical training; and, in time, qualified personnel would be available for maneuvers.[10]

In order that the Signal Corps might assume the duties of the solution of codes and ciphers and the detection of secret inks, in addition to those formerly held, certain changes were recommended in existing *Army Regulations*. The pertinent paragraph in the Communications Section of the *Handbook for War Department General Staff* (October 1923)[11] was amended to read as follows:

> This section is charged with the formulation of War Department policies relative to codes and ciphers and with the supervision of all means of secret and confidential communications in the Army. It supervises the preparation of codes and ciphers for use in peace and war and in time of war supervises the interception of enemy radio and wire traffic, the solution of enemy codes and ciphers, and the detection and employment of secret inks.[12]

Among the duties of the Chief Signal Officer as then currently prescribed by *Army Regulations 105-5*, 15 December 1926, was the following:

> e. The preparation and revision of the War Department Telegraph Code and other codes and ciphers required by the Army.

This paragraph was amended on 10 May 1929 as follows:

> e. The preparation and revision of all codes and ciphers required by the Army, and in time of war the interception of enemy radio and wire traffic, the goniometric location of enemy radio stations, the solution of intercepted enemy code and cipher messages, and laboratory arrangements for the employment and detection of secret inks.[13]

Though the responsibilities of the Chief Signal Officer in the field of cryptography and cryptanalysis were considerably expanded by this paragraph amendment, responsibility for printing, storing, issuing, and accounting for cryptographic materials was not yet a

---

9. Memorandum for the Chief of Staff from Colonel Ford (5 April 1929), sec. 2, par. 4.
10. Memorandum for Colonel Ford from Lieutenant Colonel Wilson (18 March 1929), par. 4.
11. Chapter iii in the *Handbook*, pp. 21-22.
12. Memorandum for the Chief of Staff from Colonel Ford, 5 April 1929, sec. iii, par. 2.
13. *Ibid.*, par. 3. Changes No. 1, 10 May 1929, to AR 105-5, 15 December 1926.

function of the Chief Signal Officer. Printing, storing, issuing, and accounting for cryptographic materials continued to remain with the Adjutant General until 1934.

CREATION OF THE SIGNAL INTELLIGENCE SERVICE

As a consequence of the transfer of cryptanalytic functions from the Military Intelligence Division, a conference, attended by Lieutenant Colonel John E. Hemphill, Major William R. Blair, Major O.S. Albright, and Mr. William F. Friedman, was held in the Office of the Chief Signal Officer on 19 July 1929. At this conference, the conclusion was reached that the primary function of the newly formed Signal Intelligence Service[14] was one of training personnel for utilization in time of war and of establishing the necessary organization to accomplish the training missions of the respective sections of the Signal Intelligence Service.[15]

It was proposed that the Signal Intelligence Service should consist of four sections, organized in a unified manner and administered by the Office of the Chief Signal Officer. These were to be:

      a.   Code and Cipher Compilation
      b.   Code and Cipher Solution
      c.   Intercept and Goniometry
      d.   Secret Ink

The function of the Code and Cipher Compilation Section was to continue the policy formulated ten years previously. Codes and ciphers were to be produced for use in peace, but a certain number of reserve codes and ciphers were to be kept ready for immediate use in time of war. The peacetime mission included training of cryptographic personnel who would be able to function properly in the field during war.

The Code and Cipher Solution Section was to be trained and organized for a war-type emergency. In such a crisis it would be capable of solving enemy codes and ciphers. Thus, its work was to be primarily the establishment of a training program,

---

14. The term "signal intelligence" had been coined a few days previously by Mr. Friedman. Though the new agency was known officially as the Signal Intelligence Service, a designation it was to retain until 1942, it appears on various Tables of Organization of the War Plans and Training Division, Office of the Chief Signal Officer (e.g. 15 October 1934 — SPSIS 320.3; 2 March 1937 — *ibid.*) as the "Signal Intelligence Section," a designation which was also used in the title of some of the technical papers published by the organization prior to 1937.

15. Memorandum (minutes of the Conference — SPSIS 320.3), p. 1.

not the immediate interception and solution of the communications of foreign armies or governments. If, however, in the course of the training program, foreign messages were intercepted and solved, and if they were found to contain material of potential value as intelligence, G-2 would be furnished the information obtained, but this was to be regarded as a by-product of the training work, not a normal function of the service in peacetime.

In time of war the principal function of the Intercept and Goniometric Section was to be the interception of enemy communications and the location of enemy transmitting stations by goniometric means.[16] In time of peace its principal objective was to be the organization and training of units which could effectively function during wartime. Similar aims were assigned to the Secret Ink section. It was to devise and develop secret inks for the use of G-2 personnel and to detect secret inks in enemy documents. Its peacetime mission was likewise one of research and training for operations in time of war.

It was contemplated that sections of the Signal Intelligence Service would be organized in the Panama and Hawaiian Departments, where training maneuvers and exercises were frequently conducted. These sections were to be manned by enlisted personnel. It was decided that higher authority would be requested to determine the advisability of establishing such a section in the Philippine Department. These departmental sections were to be organized solely as intercept stations for training purposes. Intercepted material would be analyzed, however, if the section was capable of solution. The intelligence derived would be submitted to the Department G-2 or to the Department Signal Officer for transmission to the Department G-2.

The establishment of sections of the Signal Intelligence Service outside the continental limits of the United States emphasized the need for intensive training. If the overseas sections were to have a solution capability, it was estimated that it would take a minimum of two years to train the necessary cryptanalytic personnel who would be capable of acting independently at the departments indicated. It was contemplated, however, that intercepted material which proved unsolvable would be forwarded to the Office of the Chief Signal Officer for further study. The training for both intercept and goniometric work and the study of secret inks was to be conducted at Fort Monmouth, New Jersey.

---

16. A goniometer (lit. a device for measuring angles) is today more commonly known as a direction finder. Locating the source of an electrical emission, usually a radio transmitter, by means of one or more direction finders is termed getting a "fix." WGB

CLOSING OF THE CIPHER BUREAU

The transfer of code and cipher solution activities and secret ink activities involved the dissolution of the Cipher Bureau, also known as MI-8, and an abandonment of its mission except insofar as the Signal Intelligence Service assumed the functions. The Cipher Bureau under the leadership of Yardley had been designed to "obtain information of present, immediate value," but as Major Albright had discovered, little attention had been devoted to training for war.

There still remained the problem of the disposition of the personnel of the Cipher Bureau, which was made especially difficult by the withdrawal of financial support for its operations by the State Department. War Department funds were not available to cover the loss of the State Department's contribution. Until ways and means could be worked out to obtain an increase in War Department annual funds, it was suggested that the Chief of the Cipher Bureau (Herbert O. Yardley) be offered a temporary position in the Signal Intelligence Service at a salary considerably lower than that which he had previously received[17] and that other personnel of the Cipher Bureau should also be offered temporary positions, the total expenditure to be within the available funds of $10,000. Since it was considered unlikely that the offer to Mr. Yardley would be accepted by him, nor would any of the few remaining Cipher Bureau employees accept employment at lower salaries with the Signal Intelligence Service, a reorganization without "entanglements from the past" could be expected.

If this proved to be the case, four selected new individuals would be employed and given cryptographic and cryptanalytic training with the ultimate objective of becoming chiefs of Signal Intelligence departments. The four would be college graduates and great care would be taken with respect to their selection. It was anticipated also that they would qualify as reserve officers, so that, as holders of Signal Corps reserve commissions, they would be competent to act at some future date as heads, perhaps, of Signal Intelligence Service military units, wherever and whenever these might be established.

It was estimated that with the funds available from the Military Intelligence Division, which amounted to $10,000,[18] and the $7,160, paid by the Signal Corps for two persons in the Code and Cipher Section, only $1,720 additionally would be

---

17. His salary in 1929 was $7500 a year. Mr. Friedman in the same period was being paid $5600 a year. It should be remembered that at this time Yardley had not yet become *persona non grata* to the signal intelligence services of the Government. He did not publish *The American Black Chamber,* as described on pages 133-143 of *The History of Codes and Ciphers in the United States During the Period Between the World Wars, Part I. 1919-1929,* until 1931, more than a year later.

18. After the State Department had withdrawn its support.

needed to provide the total sum of $18,800, the amount necessary for the salaries of the four selected cryptanalysts and the three clerks who would serve under Mr. W.F. Friedman, the civilian Chief of the Service. The section would be assigned to the War Plans and Training Division of the Office of the Chief Signal Officer, the same division to which the Code and Cipher Section had belonged.

On 1 November 1929 the lease and salaries of the Cipher Bureau were terminated; and in October, Mr. Friedman was sent to New York to take over the files and records of the Cipher Bureau, which had been packed, and to supervise their transportation to Washington. At that time Mr. Friedman also made offers of employment in the Signal Service at Large to two of the persons who had been working in the Cipher Bureau. Mrs. Ruth Willson,[19] then the Japanese expert in the Cipher Bureau, was unable to accept a position because it involved her moving to Washington — she had a husband and child in New York. Another employee, Mr. Victor Weiskopf, had a rare-stamp business in New York, and he, too, refused the move to Washington. Other clerical employees of the Cipher Bureau were not technically trained and could not be transferred to the Signal Service at Large because they had no Civil Service status. An offer of temporary employment was made to Mr. Yardley, but he refused it.[20] Eight months later, on 1 June 1930, a second tender of appointment as a Cryptanalyst at $312.50 per month was made to Mr. Yardley, but this also was declined.[21]

OFFICIAL ESTABLISHMENT OF THE SIGNAL INTELLIGENCE SERVICE

By order of the Secretary of War, The Adjutant General officially notified the Chief Signal Officer of the changes in War Department policies relating to codes, ciphers, secret inks, radio interception, and goniometry. The text of The Adjutant General's notification was substantially that drafted by Major Albright and Mr. Friedman and is so important that it should be quoted in full:[22]

---

19. In available records she is referred to as "Ruth Willson." No reference to her as a married woman is extant.

20. Friedman, *History of the Signal Intelligence Service*, p. 11.

21. Memorandum for the Executive Officer from Edward Barnett, Civilian Assistant, 30 January 1939, Sec. II, p. 7. The salary offered Yardley was fifty percent of what he had been getting in 1929.

22. Quoted from the copy on file in the Office of the Director of Communications Research. This bears the stamp of the Office of the Chief Signal Officer, dated 1017 hours, 24 April 1930. See File AG 311.5 (4-14-30) Pub.

SUBJECT: Codes, Ciphers, Secret Inks, Radio Interception and Goniometry

TO: THE CHIEF SIGNAL OFFICER

1.   With reference to the responsibilities devolving upon the Chief Signal Officer in accordance with Army Regulations 105-5, and Changes No. 1 thereto, dated May 10, 1929, the following statement of War Department policies is transmitted.

2.   a.   Army Regulations 105-5 as amended by Changes No. 1 places the responsibility for the following activities upon the Chief Signal Officer:

(1)   Code and Cipher Compilation.
(2)   Code and Cipher Solution.
(3)   Interception of enemy radio and wire traffic.
(4)   Location of enemy radio transmitting stations by goniometric means.
(5)   Laboratory arrangements for the employment and detection of secret inks.

b.   The fundamental reason for placing the responsibility for these duties upon the Chief Signal Officer is that all correlated duties in connection with secret communication may be assigned to one operating agency for efficiency of operation.   To serve this purpose these duties will be organized by the Chief Signal Officer into a single coordinated service.

c.   Within the discretion of the Chief Signal Officer it is suggested that "Signal Intelligence Service" be the designation for this coordinated service.

3.   The general mission of this service is, and for all other military services, the proper organization and development in peacetime to the end that the service may be prepared to operate at maximum efficiency in war.

4.   The specific missions of this service may be stated as follows:

a.   The preparation and revision of all codes, ciphers and other means of secret communication to be employed by the Army in time of peace and war.

Note: In this connection it should be noted that in accordance with current Army Regulations this office[23] is responsible for the printing of codes and ciphers, for their distribution in accordance with distribution tables prepared by the Chief Signal Officer, and for their accounting.

b.   In time of war the interception of enemy communications by electrical means, the location of enemy radio transmitting stations by goniometric means; and in peacetime the necessary organization and training of personnel and the necessary development of equipment to render this service capable of immediate operation in war.

c.   In time of war the solution of all secret or disguised enemy messages or other documents that may be intercepted by the Army, or forwarded by other agencies to the Army for solution; and in peacetime the necessary research work, and the organization and training of personnel to render this service capable of immediate operation in time of war.

d.   Laboratory arrangements for the detection of intercepted enemy documents written in secret ink, and for the selection and preparation of secret inks to be employed by authorized agents of our own forces in time of war; and in peacetime the necessary research work to render this service capable of immediate operation in war.

---

23.   Office of The Adjutant General.

5. Signal Intelligence units will be organized with the following missions:

a. *Under the War Department:*

(1) The preparation of all means of secret communication employed by the Army in peace and war including secret inks, except that, upon its organization GHQ will begin the preparation of field codes and ciphers required for current replacement for subordinate units.

(2) The interception of enemy communications by electrical means, including the necessary goniometric work incident thereto.

(3) The detection and solution of secret or disguised enemy communications including those written in code, cipher, secret ink or those employing other means for disguisement.

b. *At General Headquarters:*

(1) The preparation of field codes and ciphers which are employed by subordinate units to replace those previously prepared under the War Department during peacetime.

(2) The interception of enemy communications by electrical means.

(3) The location of enemy radio transmitting stations by goniometric means.

(4) The detection and solution of secret or disguised enemy communications including those written in code, cipher, secret ink, or those employing other means of disguisement.

c. *At Headquarters of Field Armies:*

(1) The interception of enemy communications by electrical means.

(2) The location of enemy radio transmitting stations by goniometric means.

(3) The solution of intercepted enemy code or cipher messages by the assistance of cipher keys and solved codes as furnished by the service at General Headquarters.

6. Based upon the policies expressed above the Chief Signal Officer will submit at a conveniently early date a recommended draft for an Army Regulation to cover the functions and duties of this service. He will also take the necessary steps to draw up such additional regulations to cover the activities of this service as he deems appropriate for publication.

7. Peacetime Objectives:

In addition to the provisions expressed above, efforts to attain ultimate peacetime objectives with reference to certain activities of this service will be made by the Chief Signal Officer as outlined in the following paragraphs.

a. *Code Compilation*

(1) The ultimate aim of this activity is the preparation of authorized codes, satisfactory in character and sufficient in the number of copies and editions, for employment by the Army during both peace and war. Upon the outbreak of war it will become necessary for purposes of secrecy to change certain characteristics of the codes employed during peace, and the required number of copies of each code will be greatly increased. Since the preparation and publication of codes requires considerable time, it would be improvident to wait till the outbreak of war to begin this work.

(2)   Therefore, as a peacetime objective, the Chief Signal Officer will make the necessary arrangements to the end that as funds become available there will be at all times in the possession of this office for immediate distribution one edition of each authorized secret code, with cipher tables if necessary, and in the possession of the Chief Signal Officer two reserve editions of such codes and cipher tables.

b.   *Code and Cipher Solution*

(1)   The ultimate peacetime objective of this activity is the training of sufficient personnel to the end that they will be expert in solving enemy code and cipher messages in war. It is also evident that much time will be required for this training. Also, since large commands require the operation of this activity in the conduct of their peacetime training, it is necessary that it operate for them during their training exercises, such as during the Joint Army and Navy Maneuvers held periodically in the Hawaiian and Panama Canal Departments and on the Atlantic seaboard, or during combined maneuvers in the Eighth or other Corps Areas. It is evident therefore that the peacetime organization and training of this activity should contemplate, first, training personnel, and second, furnishing specialists to large commands for peacetime maneuvers after personnel has been sufficiently trained. To accomplish this end it would seem that, at the present inception of this new service, its peacetime training should be centralized under the office of the Chief Signal Officer, and that the comparatively small number of trainer personnel required should be sent to corps areas and departments for assignment only for the period of maneuvers, and upon completion of maneuvers should be returned to the office of the Chief Signal Officer. The procedure insures the necessary continuity of their initial training under the Chief Signal Officer, whose office is the only military agency at the present time qualified to carry it on. However, each corps area or department which requires this service should be in a position ultimately to function independently with reference to it. It would seem therefore that the Chief Signal Officer should be prepared to furnish trained specialists of this service for permanent assignment to such corps areas and departments as the War Department may later decide, when the training has progressed to such extent that sufficient personnel are able to function as independent units.

(2)   The peacetime organization and training of this service will be based on the procedure as indicated above.

c.   *Radio Intercept*

(1)   This activity is very closely related in its operation to code and cipher solution, in that the interception of enemy messages answers no purpose unless the messages are solved, and on the other hand, the solution service depends primarily upon the activities of the intercept service for work material. It is evident therefore that the operation of both services should be carried on in close liaison. Hence the ultimate training of both services involves mutually coordinated operation.

(2)   The chief peacetime problems confronting the radio intercept service are first, the development of equipment, and second, the development of the technique of the operating personnel. The second is incident to the first and may be considered as one with it. It is evident that there is the same need for this service as for the code and cipher solution service in the peacetime maneuvers of large commands. It is also a possibility that during peacetime or during periods of strained relations the War Department or Commanders of Departments and of certain corps areas may desire the operation of this service, provided the services of a code and cipher solution agency can be made available. It is also evident that the practical operation of this service is regional and cannot be concentrated in any locality as can the code and cipher solution service. In other words, intercept stations must be located at certain critical points

where their operation may be effective, such as within departments or certain corps areas, while the code and cipher solution service may be located in Washington or any other place, provided proper communication facilities may be made available between the two services.

(3)   It would seem therefore that the peacetime activity of the radio intercept service should be directed toward objectives stated in chronological sequence as follows:

(a)   The development of equipment directly under the Chief Signal Officer.

(b)   The location of an intercept station to be prepared to operate directly under the Chief Signal Officer.

(c)   When equipment has been developed and obtained in sufficient quantity, the location of stations at critical points as follows, in the Hawaiian, Panama Canal and Philippine Departments, and in the Eighth and Ninth Corps Areas; these stations to operate under the department and corps area commanders concerned; the Chief Signal Officer to recommend when such stations should be established, at which time the matter will be taken up by the War Department with department and corps area commanders concerned.

(4)   It is contemplated that:

(a)   Should certain interceptions be desired by the War Department, which condition does not exist at the present time, the Chief Signal Officer will be called upon to recommend what station or stations can best perform the service, and the War Department will issue necessary instructions.

(b)   Should interceptions be desired by department or corps area commanders concerned, they will obtain them by means of the facilities under their control.

(c)   Messages in code or cipher intercepted by stations under the control of the Chief Signal Officer will be transmitted for solution to the code and cipher solution service operating under him.

(d)   Messages in code or cipher intercepted by stations under the control of department or corps area commanders will be transmitted by mail to the War Department for solution by the code and cipher solution section operating under the Chief Signal Officer until such time as a code an cipher solution service shall have been established under the control of the department or corps area commanders concerned.

d.   *Goniometry*

Goniometric work and its results may be considered as divided into two phases, one which is supplemental to radio interception, and one which gives the location of enemy radio transmitting stations and thus indicates the enemy's tactical disposition. The work of these two phases, while serving two different purposes, is performed by the same or similar equipment and personnel. The chief peacetime problem of the goniometric service is the same as that of the radio intercept service, namely, the development of suitable equipment and methods. These close relations between the goniometric service and the radio intercept service indicates that a basis of peacetime activities similar to that stated for the radio intercept service should be adopted for the goniometric service, and that the development of equipment, the organization and training of personnel, and the location of stations of the goniometric service should be carried out in a manner similar to that of the radio intercept service as outlined in paragraph *c.* above.

e. *Secret Inks*

The peacetime objectives of activities in connection with secret inks
is the establishment of a small laboratory for the conduct of research work which will
result in the wartime objectives of the establishment of an agency for the detection of
secret inks employed by the enemy, and for the recommendation of suitable secret inks
to be employed by authorized agents of our own forces.

By order of the Secretary of War:

/s/ Alfred J. Booth
Adjutant General

In accordance with the directive from the Secretary of War a draft was immediately formulated for *Army Regulations* to cover the functions and duties of the Signal Intelligence Service. Five types of signal intelligence units were to be organized, (1) in the War Department, (2) in the corps areas and departments, (3) at General Headquarters, (4) with the field armies, and (5) Radio Intelligence Companies which might be assigned to any of the spheres of activity outside of the War Department.[24]

While the War Department Signal Intelligence Service was designed to operate directly under the control of the Chief Signal Officer, general staff supervision of its activities was exercised by the G-2 division of the War Department General Staff. The signal intelligence units in the corps areas or departments were established at the direction of the War Department, but operated under direct control of the local Signal Officer, under the general staff supervision of the corps area or department G-2.[25]

The General Headquarters organization included a Signal Intelligence Service and several Radio Intelligence Companies under its supervision and direction. Since the sphere of the General Headquarters' Signal Intelligence Service was in a theater of operations, its duties included the study of captured enemy documents relating to enemy signal communications which were forwarded to it by the G-2 division of the General Headquarters general staff. It was composed of four sections, devoted to administration, radio intelligence, security, secret inks, the compilation of codes and ciphers, and the solution of enemy codes and ciphers.[26]

The Army Signal Intelligence Service was to consist of a headquarters section, with one or more Radio Intelligence Companies operating under its direction and supervision. The duties of this unit were restricted to the combat zone, including

24. Organization and the Duties of the Signal Intelligence Service (SPSIS 322) par. 2, pp. 5-6
25. *Ibid.* pars. 16-17, pp. 11-12.
26. *Ibid.* pars. 18-19, pp. 13-14.

interception, goniometry, the translation of messages with the assistance of information supplied by General Headquarters, and the supervision of radio and wire traffic to subordinate units within the field army concerned, particularly maintaining communication security within the combat zone. The four sections of the Army Signal Intelligence Service unit were engaged in administrative, solution, radio intelligence, and security activities.[27]

In its solution of enemy codes and ciphers, the Army Service unit was to prepare plans and orders for radio surveillance of enemy radio stations and interception of traffic. Intercepted traffic was to be solved, indexed, and filed, and documents and messages were to be translated. It was to exchange derived intelligence promptly with General Headquarters and adjacent armies.[28]

The Radio Intelligence Section was to issue orders for the radio surveillance of its sector of the combat zone for interception and the location and grouping of enemy stations by goniometry. Intercepted traffic was to be submitted to the code and cipher section for translation and for transmittal to General Headquarters for study and solution. This section was also to correlate, evaluate, and submit in proper form all information obtained concerning the location and grouping of enemy radio stations, call signs, operating frequencies, transmitting and operating characteristics to permit useful inferences to be drawn therefrom.[29] It monitored United States Army communications for security reasons and supervised the training and operation of the Army Radio Intelligence Company.[30]

The principal aim of the Security Section was to intercept communications from friendly radio stations in order to discover violations of cryptographic security rules and regulations. Radio camouflage was to be used for the deception of the enemy. It was to also maintain surveillance to prevent the tapping of our important wire lines and to tap enemy wire circuits. Reports concerning violations of cryptographic and communication security were to be submitted as required and information gleaned from tapping enemy wire circuits was to be compiled for forwarding.[31]

The fifth Signal Intelligence Service unit was the Radio Intelligence Company. It

---

27. *Ibid.* pars. 21-22, p. 18.
28. *Ibid.* par. 23, p. 19. It is to be noted that the evaluation of information and the dissemination of the thereby derived intelligence were at that time contemplated to be an assigned function of the Signal Intelligence service — an important point, since these functions usually belonged to Military Intelligence.
29. Today this is known as traffic analysis. WGB
30. *Ibid.*
31. *Ibid.* par. 23, p. 26.

was "equipped to perform intercept and goniometric functions for both limited and long range enemy transmission." The proper disposition and location of personnel and equipment for satisfactory interception was considered a matter of critical importance. Its coordination by the Army Signal Officer was essential, but considerable latitude and freedom of action on the part of the operating personnel were highly desirable in order that interception might be timely and accurate.[32]

In all cases the general mission of the Radio Intelligence company consisted of the interception of enemy radio traffic, the location of enemy transmitting stations, and the surveillance of our own radio transmissions for purposes of security; but its principal mission depended on the purpose for which it was employed. It was not organized to intercept enemy wire or visual signal traffic. Its organization, training, and equipment were under five categories:

(1) As a unit of the GHQ Signal Service;
(2) As a unit of the Field Army Signal Service;
(3) In coastal frontier defense;
(4) For border surveillance;
(5) For interior surveillance.[33]

In organization, at war strength, the Radio Intelligence Company consisted of a headquarters and three operating platoons. The headquarters platoon consisted of an administrative section for company administration and mess; a supply and transportation section, which also repaired radio equipment; and an intercept section. The latter was to operate in two teams, each composed of four intercept stations. Its primary function was to intercept enemy traffic and to monitor Army communications, and to report enemy identifications and frequencies.[34]

The operating platoon was to consist of an intercept section, a control section, and a position finding section. Their operations were interrelated so that the entire platoon operated as a team primarily for the purpose of intercepting and locating enemy radio transmitting stations. The intercept section operated four radio receiving stations and located targets by direction finding and served as an intercept unit. The control section assigned missions to the intercept and position finding sections and consolidated information and transmitted it to the company command post. It also installed and maintained the telephone systems required by the platoons, providing the tie lines necessary to connect them with the company and higher

---

32. *Ibid.* par. 24a, p. 21.
33. *Ibid.* par. 24b, p. 21.
34. *Ibid.* par. 24c, p. 21.

headquarters. The position finding section operated four direction-finding stations to locate enemy radio transmitting stations by radio goniometric methods.[35] The duties of the various platoons varied with their assignments.[36]

SIGNAL INTELLIGENCE SERVICE PERSONNEL

Although the official sanction for the transfer of the functions of the Cipher Bureau to the Chief Signal Officer was embodied in the change of Army Regulations dated 10 May 1929, the actual termination of the Cipher Bureau as a distinct organization did not occur until 1 November 1929, and the Chief Signal Officer was not officially advised, as has been stated, of the policies that had been formulated until he received The Adjutant General's letter of 22 April 1930. Meanwhile, however, steps had been initiated to employ the necessary personnel after the appropriations from the Military Intelligence Division became available. On 16 December 1929, the sum of $6,666.68 was allotted by the Assistant Chief of Staff, G-2, to the Chief Signal Officer for the payment of personnel engaged in code and cipher work.[37]

Provision had already been made for the cryptanalyst and the clerk authorized for the Code and Cipher Section of the Chief Signal Officer. It was necessary, however, to select and employ the personnel who were to be trained as permanent members of the Signal Intelligence Service. On 4 January 1930, the Secretary of War was requested by the Chief Signal Officer to authorize the employment of four Junior cryptanalysts (P-1) at $2,000 a year and one assistant cryptographic clerk (CAF-3) at $1,620 a year in the Signal Service at Large, Washington, D.C. They were to engage in the preparation of codes and ciphers, because it had been concluded that there should "be established during peacetime a small section of code and cipher specialists who will be under constant training in these sciences." These experts were to keep abreast of progress in this field and would serve as a nucleus in the initial phases of any emergency for the expansion of the Signal Intelligence Service into a much larger organization for wartime. This recommendation was approved by the Secretary of War on 13 January 1930.[38]

The four junior cryptanalysts were to complete a special course of instruction in cryptanalysis. After the initial phase of their instruction had been completed, they

---

35. *Ibid.*

36. *Ibid.* par. 25, p. 22.

37. P/A MID P 5205A 1110-0. Cf. Memorandum for the Executive Officer from Edward Barnett, Civilian Assistant (30 January 1939), p. 4.

38. *Ibid.* pp. 4-5; Memorandum for the Secretary of War from the Chief Signal Officer, 4 January 1930; 1st Ind., 13 January 1930.

were to assist in the technical phases of the work of the Signal Intelligence Service: compiling codes, preparing ciphers and cipher tables, conducting research in new cryptographic methods and machinery and in the solution of codes and ciphers, and participating in field training exercises in the wartime operation of code and cipher solution units. The assistant cryptographic clerk was to perform similar duties under more immediate supervision.[39]

A restricted budget demanded that the Signal Intelligence Service be organized with a small staff. It was essential, therefore, that the four persons to be trained be carefully selected. The principal qualifications of the persons to be selected included a thorough training in mathematics and languages, embracing an understanding of French, Spanish, German, and Japanese.

Eight candidates were recommended by the Civil Service Commission, but only three of these were appointed. The three were Frank B. Rowlett,[40] appointed 1 April 1930; Abraham Sinkov,[41] appointed 10 April 1930; and Solomon Kullback,[42] appointed 21 April 1930. Miss Louise Newkirk (later Mrs. Nelson) had been appointed to the clerical vacancy on 1 March 1930.[43]

On 30 April 1930 authority was requested to employ a cryptanalyst aide (SP-5) at $1,800 a year, Signal Service at Large.[44] This recommendation was approved by the Secretary of War on 1 May 1930. Two weeks later, on 13 May 1930, Mr. John B. Hurt,[45] was appointed to this position. The Civil Service Commission, having no

---

39. Memorandum for the Secretary of War from the Chief Signal Officer, 4 January 1930.

40. Colonel Rowlett was Chief, General Cryptanalytic Branch, SSA, from 1943 to 1945 when he became Chief, Intelligence Division, afterwards the Operations Division, Army Security Agency. He reverted to inactive duty on 1 May 1946.

41. Colonel Sinkov was Commanding Officer, Central Bureau, Brisbane, from 1942 to 1945, when he returned to the U.S. In 1946 he became Chief, Security Division, Army Security Agency. He was on active duty in June 1946.

42. Colonel Kullback was Chief, Military Cryptanalytic Branch, SSA, from 1943 to 1945 when he became Chief, Research and Development Division, Army Security Agency. He reverted to inactive duty on 1 June 1946.

43. Executive Officer, Office of the Chief Signal Officer, to Secretary, Fourth U.S. Civil Service District, 25 February 1930; Memorandum for the executive Officer from Edward Barnett, Civilian Assistant, 30 January 1939, p. 6.

44. Several years earlier Mr. Friedman, jointly with the Chief of the Code and Cipher Section of the Navy Department, had drawn up a schedule of job descriptions, in order to keep both services aligned in respect to qualifications, grades, rates of pay, etc., of cryptographic and cryptanalytic personnel. This farsighted move was to become quite important later on.

45. From that date Mr. Hurt remained an employee of the Signal Intelligence Service or of its successors. During World War II Mr. Hurt worked at different times in the Military Cryptanalytic Branch or the Language Branch.

eligible mathematicians who also knew Japanese available, waived in this case the usual procedure for employment, thus permitting the War Department to fill the position with Mr. Hurt whose knowledge of Japanese was outstanding.[46] One additional vacancy remained to be filled; and on 2 September 1930 Lawrence Clark[47] was appointed assistant cryptographic clerk (CAF-3) at $1,620 a year.

The work of the Signal Intelligence Service was performed by Mr. Friedman and these six assistants on a budget of from $17,060 to $17,400 a year from 1930 to the conclusion of Fiscal Year 1937. There were some changes in clerical personnel during this period, but the total remained constant. When Lawrence Clark was transferred to the Navy Department in 1935, he was replaced on 1 January 1936 by Herrick F. Bearce.[48] When Dr. Abraham Sinkov was transferred to Panama in 1936 and Dr. Solomon Kullback was transferred to Hawaii in 1937, they were replaced, respectively, by Robert O. Ferner[49] and M.A. Jones.[50]

The five years 1933-1938 marked a period of severe economic depression, not only in the Nation at large, but in the Signal Intelligence Service in particular. Promotions were not made and salaries were cut. As a result, morale was low.

In Fiscal Year 1938, as the tension in a militant Europe became more evident, the authorization for personnel in the Signal Intelligence Service was increased to eleven: two additional junior cryptanalysts and two more clerks were added. The budget for the Signal Intelligence Service was raised to $24,360 for that year.[51] After the Munich crisis, when conflict appeared inevitable, the authorization for the Fiscal Year 1939 was increased to fourteen persons.[52]

---

46. Memorandum for the Executive Officer, Office of the Chief Signal Officer, from Major D.M. Crawford (29 April 1930).

47. Lieutenant Colonel Clark later was on the staff of Colonel Sinkov in Australia. Later he became Assistant Chief, Security Division, Army Security Agency.

48. Lieutenant Colonel Bearce served with signal intelligence units in North Africa, Italy, France, and Germany during World War II. In April 1946 he became chief of one of the large sections of the Intelligence Division, Army Security Agency.

49. Mr. Ferner continued to be employed as a cryptanalyst during World War II. In 1946 he was a member of the Research and Development Division, Army Security Agency. Mr. Jones and Mrs. Nelson were the only employees of this early period who did not remain throughout the war.

50. Memorandum for the Executive Officer from Edward Barnett, 30 January 1939, p. 7.

51. For the first time in the history of the Signal Intelligence Service, the budget approximated the lowest sum spent by Yardley's Cipher Bureau in any one year. It should be mentioned that the increase in Fiscal Year 1938 of additional personnel for signal intelligence work was the first in the War Department's preparations for expansion and possible war.

52. Memorandum for the Executive Officer from Edward Barnett, 30 January 1939.

CONCLUSION

The unification of units engaged in the solution of secret means of communication with those assigned the task of code and cipher compilation marked a progressive step in the development of cryptological activity in the War Department. Training for war had become the fundamental objective of the Signal Intelligence Service. Even that training, however, as well as the other essential work of the organization, was handicapped by the program of economy imposed on the War Department in a period of economic depression and budgetary restriction.

In October 1931, during preparation of the budget for Fiscal Year 1934, it was recommended by the Chief Signal Officer that personnel for the solution of codes and ciphers should be increased by four. Such an expansion was deemed necessary for the proper discharge of this function if the Army was to have trained Signal Intelligence personnel available for mobilization of necessary sections on M-Day. The proposal would have increased personnel to eleven and the budget to $24,740 by 1934, but as we have seen the actual authorization for that increase was not obtained until 1938.[53]

The entire burden for the support of Signal Intelligence activities was thrown upon the Signal Corps in Fiscal Year 1932 when the Military Intelligence Division allotment was withdrawn. The Signal Corps therefore increased its allotment to the Signal Intelligence Service by $9,600 to make up for the loss of the G-2 appropriation. Though the Signal Corps had many other operations to support, the importance of the Signal Intelligence Service was fully appreciated.[54]

In 1935 the Chief of the Signal Intelligence Service recommended that the time had come to expand the Signal Intelligence activities in the Office of the Chief Signal Officer. It was recommended that the Signal Intelligence Service be organized on a more extensive basis, "in order that personnel for efficient operations may be available when the situation will require their services." It was considered essential to provide opportunities for advancement for the personnel already employed, in order that a restricted field might be attractive to them. Otherwise, the Signal Intelligence Service might "become merely a training ground for other departments."[55]

---

53. Memorandum for The Adjutant General from Executive Officer, OCSigO, Subject: *Signal Intelligence Service, 14 October 1931* (SPSIS 311.5).

54. *Ibid.*, Inclosure.

55. Memorandum to Major Rumbough from W.F. Friedman, 19 August 1935 (SPSIS 320.2).

A five-year expansion program was recommended which would increase the total personnel to 21 by 1942, with a total budget of $54,660.[56] Several obstacles impeded the immediate approval of this plan. In the first place, any proposal for an increase in salaries of personnel in the Signal Intelligence Service was held to be objectionable. For several years, owing principally to economy measures imposed by the President and Congress, it had not been possible to provide administrative promotions for any Signal Corps employees. Moreover, the President had directed that no promotions were to be included in the 1937 budget.[57]

A second obstacle was that the personnel and equipment assigned to the Signal Intelligence Service already fully occupied its available space and because of the existing critical shortage of office and storage space in the District of Columbia no additional space was likely to be found for any possible expansion of the organization. It was suggested that additions to the existing force would overcrowd their present working area, being a detriment to health and comfort as well as impairing the performance of their duties.[58]

The request for additional Signal Intelligence Service personnel was not approved and the four new positions had to be deleted from the estimates. One of the contributory factors which necessitated this was the lack of support received from representatives of G-2. Assurance had been obtained from G-2 in advance that it would cooperate in defense of the increase, but its representatives "failed to appear at the hearing when held."[59]

It was the opinion of Major W.S. Rumbough, Officer in Charge of the War Plans and Training Division, of which the Signal Intelligence Service was a part, that "a serious shortage of trained personnel exists in the Signal Intelligence Service" such that it could not "fully perform its peacetime mission." If this shortage should "be allowed to continue, no Signal Intelligence Service worthy of the name would be available during the early phase of an emergency when the most valuable results should be expected from this agency."[60]

---

56. By 1942 war had been declared and the budget actually increased many times over the figure requested.

57. Routing and Work Sheet, 19 December 1935, Action 2, Fiscal Officer to Executive Officer, OCSigO, no date (SPSIS 320.2).

58. Routing and Work Sheet, 19 December 1935, Action 3, Civilian Assistant to Executive Officer, OCSigO, no date (SPSIS 320.2).

59. Memorandum for the Chief Signal Officer from Major W.S. Rumbough, Subject: *Increase in Personnel for the Signal Intelligence Service,* 18 February 1936 (SPSIS 320.2).

60. *Ibid.*

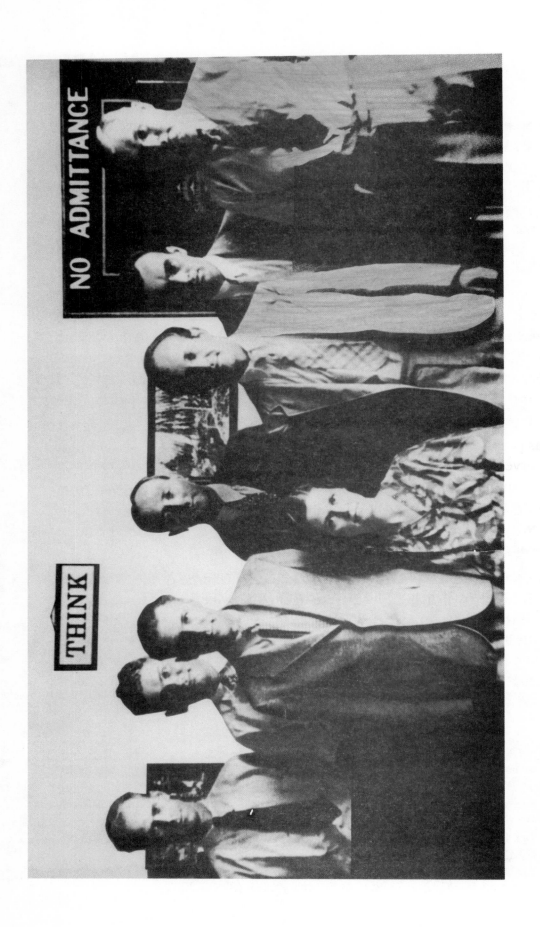

SIS CRYPTANALYSTS WHO BROKE THE PURPLE MACHINE

This classic photograph was taken shortly before World War II by Major Cansler. Shown in Room 3416 of the Munitions Building are standing, from left to right, Herrick F. Bearce, Solomon Kullback, First Lieutenant Harrod G. Miller, William F. Friedman, Abraham Sinkov, Lieutenant Leonard T. Jones, USCG, and Frank B. Rowlett. Louise Newkirk Nelson sits in front.

CHAPTER II

CRYPTOGRAPHIC PROGRESS 1930–1939

CODE PRODUCTION PROGRAM 1930–1934

The policy regarding the production of codes, which had already been formulated by the Code and Cipher Section[61] in the Twenties, was continued by the Signal Intelligence Service in 1930. In general, the goal was to keep an initial M-Day issue of every code in readiness for an emergency and two reserve issues in secret storage. Every effort was made to attain this aim as soon as funds and personnel available permitted.[62] To accomplish the goal, a schedule of priorities for code production was prepared.

In 1930 it was planned that all codes required for a war emergency, together with the necessary reserve editions,[63] would be published within the succeeding ten years. The amount to be expended for printing and binding the codes in any fiscal year never exceeded $7,600, while the number of codes to be printed in any single year varied from one to seven.[64]

Within a year, however, it became necessary to formulate a new program which would reflect the reduced budget for printing and binding upon which the compilation unit was forced to depend. The schedule of seven codes to be printed in 1931 was not fulfilled. One code which was already compiled was printed, but no new codes were published. Consequently, in the revised schedule for 1932, eleven codes were listed. Many of these were revisions of codes which were relatively low in production costs, so that the estimated expense for 1932 was $5,000. This was a five-year program in which the estimated annual costs varied from $4,100 to $5,100.[65]

---

61. See *The History of Codes and Ciphers in the United States During the Period Between the World Wars, Part I. 1919-1929*, Chapter I, pp. 1-42.

62. Memorandum for Lieutenant Colonel O.S. Albright from Major D.M. Crawford, 5 April 1930 (SPSIS 111).

63. That is, sufficient codes would be available in case of war.

64. See footnote 62, above.

65. 1st Memo. Ind. for The Adjutant General from the Chief Signal Officer, 28 April 1931 (SPSIS 111).

It was evident by March 1932 that the personnel assigned to the task of code compilation were insufficient to properly accomplish the work. The urgency of the task required to compile twelve authorized editions of codes that had yet to be prepared was such that all other activities would have to be suspended if the task were to be completed. It was estimated that it would take a single team of two junior cryptanalysts and one assistant cryptographic clerk three years to compile the needed manuscripts. If an additional code was authorized, an additional year would be required.[66]

Therefore, as early as 1933, an official revision of the code production program was considered necessary. It was submitted to the Chief of Staff and approved by Major General Hugh A. Drum, Deputy Chief of Staff, on 22 March 1933. The new program required the publication of ten codes in Fiscal Year 1935 and postponed the printing of the larger *War Department Staff Codes No. 2* and *No. 3* until the Fiscal Years 1936 and 1939, respectively. Four other codes were scheduled for Fiscal Year 1936 and three for Fiscal Year 1937. As a result, estimated costs gradually reduced from 1935, when they totalled $12,850, to $9,000 for the single volume of *War Department Staff Code No. 4* to be printed in 1939.[67]

Two additional paragraphs, requesting that The Adjutant General include the funds necessary for printing and binding the required codes in his estimates and that two additional clerks be added to the staff failed to receive the concurrence of the Assistant Chief of Staff, G-4. The latter objected because the project would cost $13,650 per year for five years and he could not concur unless that sum could be absorbed by either The Adjutant General or the Chief Signal Officer in their budgets.[68]

The revision of the code compilation program was carried even farther in the latter part of 1933. The Code Production Program of 22 March 1933 anticipated that *Army Field Code No. 2* and *Division Field Code No. 11* would be printed in Fiscal Year 1934 at a total estimated cost of $5,000. Special funds became available to The Adjutant General toward the close of Fiscal Year 1933. As a result, the Signal Intelligence Service was asked to print the available codes as rapidly as possible. It was possible to print both *Division Field Codes No. 11* and *No. 12* as well as *Military*

---

66. Memorandum to the Chief Signal Officer from Major D.M. Crawford, March 1932 (SPSIS 311.5).

67. Memorandum for the Chief of Staff from the Assistant Chief of Staff, G-2, Subject: *Program for Code Production,* 7 March 1933 (SPSIS 111).

68. Memorandum for the Assistant Chief of Staff, G-2, from the Assistant Chief of Staff, G-4, Subject: *Program for Code Production,* 10 March 1933 (SPSIS 111).

Intelligence Code No. 11 at a cost of $3,228 from 1933 funds. *Division Field Code No. 12*, however, was not scheduled to be printed until 1935 and a change in program was necessary.[69]

A further change was made in September 1933 when The Adjutant General notified the War Plans and Training Division that no funds would be available for printing codes in Fiscal Year 1934. It had been estimated that $5,000 would be required, of which the sum of $3,800 was needed for the publication of *Army Field Code No. 2.* Although this code was then 25 percent complete, its publication had to be postponed until funds could be secured.[70]

On 28 May 1934 The Adjutant General advised the Chief Signal Officer of a new peacetime policy relative to War Department codes. It was directed that, as funds became available, the Chief Signal Officer would always have in his possession, ready for immediate distribution, one edition of each authorized confidential and secret code. Cipher tables and two reserve editions of such codes and cipher tables would be printed and also held in reserve.[71]

The fairly wide distribution of all of the secret codes increased the possibility of the compromise of one or more codes, through loss, capture, or exposure as a result of carelessness in safeguarding and handling codes and messages. Even if no compromise occurred, experience had shown that the life of a secret code varied with the volume of messages sent and received and the size and type of construction of the code book. Consequently, the safest of secret communications required the substitution of a new code before the maximum permissible number of (code) groups had been transmitted. It was necessary, therefore, to insure the safety and continuity of secret communications by keeping at least two reserve editions of each code on hand at all times.[72]

In conformity with this policy, the Signal Intelligence Service concentrated its efforts on the compilation and production of the required reserve editions of all authorized secret or confidential codes.

---

69. Memorandum for Major S.B. Akin from Captain H.L.P. King, 26 February 1934 (SPSIS 311.5).

70. *Ibid.*

71. Memorandum to the Chief Signal Officer from The Adjutant General, Subject: *Codes, Ciphers, Secret Inks, Radio Interception and Goniometry,* 28 May 1934 (AG 311.5 (5-25-34) Pub.); *Annual Report of Signal Intelligence Section,* Fiscal Year 1934 (SPSIS 319.1), par. 1a.

72. Memorandum to the Assistant Chief of Staff, G-2, from Executive Officer, Office of the Chief Signal Officer, 27 February 1933 (SPSIS 111).

UNIFICATION OF CODE PRODUCTION, 1934

By 1934 it had become obvious that a complete centralization of responsibility for the production of codes and ciphers in the Office of the Chief Signal Officer was necessary in order that this work might be discharged more efficiently. The preparation of cryptographic communications involved three levels of activity. First, the Chief Signal Officer had for 14 years been charged with devising and developing the actual codes, ciphers, and cipher devices to be used by the Army. The second level of activity was that assigned to The Adjutant General. He was responsible for the publication, storage, distribution, and accounting of the codes and ciphers being used. The third level of activity was that concerned with the use of the codes and ciphers, the transmission of secret and confidential messages through their preparation and translation.[73] This level of activity was handled in each headquarters and command by personnel assigned these duties by the commander. In Washington this work was done within the Cable Section of The Adjutant General's Office, a unit which had been transferred to his jurisdiction from the General Staff in August 1921. There was nothing to be gained by making changes in regard to the third level of activity, but as regards the first and second levels, the division of responsibility for correlated or related duties between two unconnected operating agencies, i.e., the Office of the Chief Signal Officer and The Adjutant General's Office, was unsound with an attendant loss of efficiency and security.[74]

Funds for the publication of codes and ciphers were never specifically allocated for that purpose, but rather were taken out of a lump sum allotted to The Adjutant General in accordance with practical exigencies of the moment.[75] It was evident that the existing loose arrangement did not facilitate the establishment and execution of a well-conceived and consistent program for the initial issues of authorized codes and ciphers nor for the subsequent replacements of those which had grown obsolete.

The printing of codes and ciphers differed in technique from that of the majority of other War Department documents which were published by The Adjutant General.

---

73. Preparation and translation means cryptographing and decryptographing. WGB

74. Draft Memorandum to Major Wogan, G-2, Subject: *The Unification and Coordination of Cryptographic Work in the Military Establishment,* 1933 (SPSIS 311.5); Memorandum for the Chief of Staff from Brigadier General Alfred T. Smith, Subject: *War Department Policies with reference to Codes and Ciphers,* 18 December 1933 (SPSIS 311.5).

75. Draft Memorandum to Major Wogan, Par. 6a; Memorandum to the Chief of Staff from Brigadier General Smith, Sec. II, par. 1c (2).

WILLIAM F. FRIEDMAN

The contributions of William F. Friedman to the modern science of cryptology, as described in this book, clearly show why he is considered the father of the modern science of cryptology. He is the author of numerous books dealing with cryptography and cryptanalysis. See also Ronald Clark's The Man Who Broke Purple *(Little, Brown and Company, Boston, 1977).*

MUNITIONS BUILDING

The Signal Intelligence Service was located in the third wing (Room 3416) of the Munitions Building, a large, multi-winged cement building on Constitution Avenue, facing 20th Street, in Washington, D.C. In 1942 much of the War Department moved to the newly built Pentagon Building and the Signal Intelligence Service moved to Arlington Hall Station, both across the Potomac River in Arlington, Virginia.

To insure necessary security only a limited number of persons could be entrusted with the work in all of its stages, including the preparation by mimeograph or multigraph in the Office of the Chief Signal Officer.[76]

The assumption by the Chief Signal Officer of preparing cipher tables and cipher alphabets — generally to be used with already published codes — was a necessary responsibility, but it was also unauthorized. But in time of war, when cipher tables and cipher alphabets might have to be replaced at very frequent intervals, it was evident that the Signal Corps, to obviate delays, was better prepared to publish as well as to devise and to develop the necessary cipher tables and cipher alphabets. It was clear that this added responsibility accepted by the Chief Signal Officer was one that should be covered by appropriate regulations in a definite assignment of duty.[77]

After their publication, codes and ciphers had to be properly stored and distributed to authorized holders. It was essential also that there be a periodic accounting of all classified documents. In an edition of a thousand or more copies a publication might cost thousands of dollars to produce, yet be rendered entirely worthless by the loss or compromise of but a single copy.[78]

To provide adequate security, storage facilities for secret documents had to be carefully considered. The Adjutant General had no vault or storage space available which provided the degree of security necessary. Therefore, many secret codes and ciphers had to be stored in space under the control of the Chief Signal Officer. While the vault — under the control of the Chief Signal Officer — in the Munitions Building[79] was superior to the space available to The Adjutant General, it was neither secure enough nor sufficiently large for the storage of the secret codes. The vault was used for the storage of various classified documents relating to signal intelligence work. Although the Chief of the Signal Intelligence Section was the only person who knew the combination of the vault, access to it was granted of necessity to some of his assistants.[80]

The Chief Signal Officer officially was not responsible for the storage of codes and could not initiate a proposal for a new vault. On the other hand, since The Adjutant General did not actually store all of the codes, he could not adequately

---

76. Draft Memorandum to Major Wogan, par. 6c.

77. *Ibid.*

78. *Ibid.* par. 6d.

79. The Munitions Building was a large, multi-winged, cement building on Constitution Avenue, facing 20th Street. WGB

80. Draft Memorandum to Major Wogan, G-2, Subject: *The Unification and Coordination of Cryptographic Work in the Military Establishment,* 1933 (SPSIS 311.5).

defend a project for a new vault. His storeroom, on the top floor of the State, War and Navy Building, was large enough for storage of the reserve editions as published, but it was considered unsafe because it had a wooden door without a combination lock and two skylights which could easily be broken, although they were fastened down.[81]

These storage arrangements complicated the distribution of code and cipher publications within the Army. The Adjutant General, the officer authorized to control the storage of codes and ciphers under *Army Regulations,* had to call on the Chief Signal Officer to supply copies when needed. Distribution also involved accounting, exceedingly important if secret codes were not to be lost. It is suffice to say that the existing arrangement, with its divided responsibility between the Chief Signal Officer and The Adjutant General, involved a duplication of operations. It was not only considered illogical, but from the viewpoint of economy of effort and of communications security, it was believed to be untenable.[82]

As already mentioned, the third level of cryptographic activity in Army communications involves the actual handling of codes and ciphers in the transmission and reception of messages. Other operations or levels of activity are merely preliminaries to the provision of means for assuring secrecy in communications, the real purpose of codes and ciphers. Experience gained in war and peace has amply demonstrated that even the most efficient code or cipher cannot provide security if the cryptographic personnel using the system are inefficient, careless, or untrained.[83]

In military units the responsibility of cryptographing and decryptographing messages was a function of the "message center" according to *Army Regulations.* Although message center personnel received a certain amount of training in the use of codes and ciphers, additional training would have been valuable. Even in permanent headquarters, such as in those of Corps Areas or Departments, or even in the headquarters of the War Department itself, messages requiring cryptographing and decryptographing were sometimes handled by personnel to whom other and more pressing duties were also assigned and no special cryptographic training was provided. In one Corps Area the work might be performed by G-2, while in another it might be handled by G-3 or G-1.[84]

In those headquarters where secrecy in communications was most often desired and indeed where most essential, the frequent absence of properly trained personnel was

---

81. *Ibid.*, Memorandum for the Chief of Staff from Brigadier General Smith, Sec. II, par. 1d.
82. Memorandum to Major Wogan, par. 6e.
83. *Ibid.* par. 7a.
84. *Ibid.* par. 7b.

conducive to a reduction in security. Blunders in cryptography that might be of value to an enemy cryptanalyst were not always caused by carelessness. Lack of technical knowledge, which could be acquired only through special training and experience in cryptanalysis, was a fundamental cause.[85]

Procedures for the routing of secret and confidential messages also involved difficulties. In the War Department, plaintext messages were typed and forwarded to The Adjutant General's Office by messenger with the request that they be sent in an appropriate secret code. In that office, the messages were turned over to the Cable Section where personnel with little or no training in cryptanalysis then cryptographed the message. Cryptographic versions of the messages were then carried by messenger to the War Department Message Center for transmission. At their destinations the messages might finally be decryptographed by one of several staff officers, as designated by the local commander. Under such circumstances, the control of plaintext messages, either literal versions or paraphrase versions, resulted in a constant threat to security. Serious cryptographic blunders might lie undetected, because, in this routine, a trained cryptanalyst could not observe the various cryptographic clerks in actual operation.[86]

A further objection to the existing procedure was that it did not make it easy for the code-producing agency to determine the suitability of existing code systems because that agency had no opportunity to observe the system in actual operation. As a result, improvements in a system were based on purely theoretical considerations and it was very possible "that potential enemy cryptanalysts" had access to "better data concerning cryptographic idiosyncrasies of the U.S. Army" than did the Army's own code compilers.[87]

If, as was confidently anticipated, the cryptographing and decryptographing of communications at the larger headquarters were to be accomplished in the future by automatic machines, which would require trained technicians for their operation and maintenance, the feeling of the Chief Signal Officer was that these technicians should be Signal Corps specialists, performing their work at a message center under Signal Corps control.[88]

---

85. *Ibid.*

86. *Ibid.* par. 7c. In this and the previous paragraph it is pointed out that security was reduced because clerks had no special training or experience in cryptanalysis. In the years prior to World War II, when "codes" were the principal means of encrypting messages, there may perhaps have been a need for cryptographic clerks to have a certain amount of knowledge concerning cryptanalysis. Today, however, when practical cryptographic systems are generally highly secure computer-type cipher systems, the need to have cryptographic operators with a knowledge of or training in cryptanalysis is doubtful. WGB

87. *Ibid.*

88. *Ibid.*, par. 7d.

A final consideration towards effecting a transfer of all cryptographic operations to Signal Corps control lay in the responsibility for the coordination and supervision of secret communications exercised by the Military Intelligence Division. This became more difficult to fulfill with the complicated distribution of such activities. In matters pertaining to the solution of enemy codes and ciphers, G-2 had only the Signal Corps to consider, but in matters relating to the security of U.S. Army communications, it found itself in the position of having to coordinate its activities with several agencies, the Signal Corps, The Adjutant General, the various corps areas and department staffs. This situation presented a constant threat to security and impaired the efficiency of operations with no compensating advantage in economy of either time or effort.[89]

Taking these considerations into accord, it was therefore recommended to the Chief of Staff that the publication, storage, distribution, and accounting of codes and ciphers be transferred to the Signal Corps. The Chief Signal Officer was to include in his annual budget the necessary funds for printing and binding codes and ciphers, prepared in accordance with the approved program of code production. The Cable Section of the Office of The Adjutant General was to be transferred also to the Office of the Chief Signal Officer.[90]

On 21 March 1933 the Chief of the Signal Intelligence Section[91] was designated as the contact representative of the War Department for code production at the Government Printing Office.[92] This still did not eliminate the objections to the Adjutant General's control of funds for printing and binding codes, and a recommendation for the transfer of the control of such funds to the Chief Signal Officer was made on 6 February 1934.[93]

The Assistant Chief of Staff, G-4, objected to the recommendation that the control of funds for printing and binding codes and ciphers be transferred to the Chief Signal Officer on the ground that it was a mistake to isolate a single item. The reduction of funds allotted to code and cipher work could not be compensated by the use of funds in a general pool, and flexibility in the use of such funds would be lost. He recommended that beginning with Fiscal Year 1936 the Chief Signal Officer should be directed to prepare an estimate for the required funds for printing and binding codes

---

89. *Ibid.*, par. 8.

90. Memorandum to the Chief of Staff from Brigadier General Smith, Sect. III, par. 1, 3, 5.

91. See *The Origin and Development of the Army Security Agency, 1917-1947*, p. 2: "From 1929 to 1942 the organization was known as the *Signal Intelligence Service (SIS)* or the *Signal Intelligence Section, OCSigO*." WGB

92. The Secretary of War to the Public Printer, 21 March 1933 (SPSIS 311.5).

93. Memorandum to the Chief of Staff from Brigadier General Smith.

and ciphers in accordance with the approved program of code production. The Adjutant General would then be directed to omit this item from his estimates.[94] With this amendment the recommendation was approved on 28 May 1934.[95] The responsibility for the work was transferred to the Chief Signal Officer and estimates for the printing and binding of codes and ciphers were included with the regular Signal Corps printing and binding estimates for 1936.[96]

On 21 August 1934 the transfer of the control of the publication, storage, distribution, and accounting of all codes and ciphers from The Adjutant General's Office to the Signal Intelligence Section, Office of the Chief Signal Officer, was officially approved and a corresponding change was made in *Army Regulations*.[97] When these duties were transferred, some 20,000 publications, together with records pertaining to them, were inventoried and moved from storage rooms in the State, War and Navy Building. The publications were either placed in vaults within the Office of the Chief Signal Officer or shipped to Brooklyn for storage in the Signal Corps Depot. The transfer of the publications was performed without the loss of a single document.[98]

The transfer of storage, issue, and accounting to the Chief Signal Officer involved numerous details. *Army Regulations* required semi-annual reports from holders of code and cipher systems to be made on 30 June and 31 December. Each report had to be checked against the records to verify its accuracy and to ascertain whether all holders had reported. Names of custodians and dates of the reports had to be entered on the records. The work entailed much correspondence, since a number of holders failed to submit reports entirely, or omitted some of the items which had been issued to them.

In Fiscal Year 1935 a new system of accounting for code and cipher publications was instituted. New accounting forms were adopted, printed and distributed. Better security was established for these important documents both in the field and in Washington. The system of accounting for registered documents was facilitated by assigning short titles to the publications in accordance with Paragraph 3, AR 330-5. This system was inaugurated in the latter part of 1934 and was adopted therefore as standard

---

94. Memorandum for the Assistant Chief of Staff, G-2, from the Assistant Chief of Staff, G-4, Subject: *War Department Policies with reference to Codes and Ciphers*, 16 February 1934 (SPSIS 311.5).

95. The Adjutant General to the Chief Signal Officer through the Chief of Finance, Subject: *War Department Policies with reference to Codes and Ciphers*, 28 May 1934 (SPSIS 311.5).

96. Memorandum to the Budget Officer for the War Department from the Acting Chief Signal Officer, Subject: *Revised Estimated, Printing and Binding, Fiscal Year 1936,* 18 September 1934 (SPSIS 111).

97. Changes No. 1, to AR 105-5, 15 March 1933, 21 August 1934 AG 311-5 (25 May 1934).

98. Secret Supplement to the Annual Report of the Chief Signal Officer, 27 August 1935, (OCSigO 319.1) Sec. II, par. 1a.

for the entire War Department. Two storage vaults were set aside specifically for codes and a system of guarding and inspecting these vaults was instituted. New duties for the Signal Corps were assumed and improvements made without additional personnel.[99]

A change in the control of cryptographic operations in connection with the cryptographing and decryptographing of messages within the War Department was also approved and effected in accordance with a recommendation made to the Chief of Staff. The Code and Cable Section was transferred from The Adjutant General's Office to the War Department Message Center, and the Chief Signal Officer became responsible for all cryptographing and decryptographing in the War Department. Signal Corps officers assumed the same responsibility in corps areas and department headquarters. On 1 September 1934 *Army Regulations* were issued providing instructions for the employment of codes and ciphers and transferring telegraph, cable, and radio service functions from The Adjutant General to the Chief Signal Officer.[100]

Responsibility for the Cable Section was assumed by the Chief Signal Officer, but sufficient personnel were not available to provide for 24-hour operation[101] nor for emergencies. The Signal Intelligence Service therefore was asked to assist in training additional personnel for the efficient operation of the War Department Message Center.[102]

INTRODUCTION OF TABULATING MACHINES

One of the most important achievements in code production by the Signal Intelligence Service was the introduction of automatic methods of compilation. IBM tabulating machinery was introduced as a labor-saving device. The machines came into use somewhat by accident. Another branch of the War Department (Office of the Quartermaster General) had been using the IBM machines for tabulating purposes for some time, when a new officer-in-charge suddenly decided to stop using the machines. Although the rental agreement contract with IBM could have been terminated at once, the Chief of the Signal Intelligence Service[103] was able to persuade the Office of the Quartermaster General to allow the Signal Intelligence

---

99. *Ibid., passim.*

100. AR 105-25, Signal Corps, Telegraph, Cable, and Radio Service, 1 September 1934.

101. From this it appears that at least the Cable Section of the War Department Message Center in 1934 was not operational 24 hours a day. WGB

102. Secret Supplement to the Annual Report of the Chief Signal Officer, 27 August 1935 (OCSigO 319.1) par. 7.

103. William F. Friedman. WGB

Service to use the unexpired contracted time, which amounted to several months. The IBM machines were therefore moved to a working area of the Signal Intelligence Service where they were used for the balance of their rental period.

The experiment proved so successful that when the year's lease was about to expire, it was requested that funds be made available to continue the lease for another year. In the files of the Machine Branch, Signal Security Agency,[104] a routing slip still extant contains the following note, familiarly signed by William F. Friedman with the letter F, which accompanied the request for funds:

> Major Akin: In many years service here I have never once "set my heart on" getting something I felt desirable. But in this case I have set my heart on the matter because of the tremendous load it would lift off all our backs. The basic idea of using machinery for code compilation is mine and is of several years standing. The details of the proposed system were developed in collaboration with Mr. Case, of the International Business Machines Corporation. I regard this as one of my most important and most valuable contributions to the promotion of the work for which we are responsible. Please do your utmost for me. If you do, we can *really* begin to do worthwhile *cryptanalytic* work. F.[105]

The machines were rented from the International Business Machines Corporation at an annual rental of $600 which provided three machines, a punch, sorter and tabulator. The installation of the machines as an official charge against the budget of the Signal Intelligence Service took place on 1 February 1935.[106] Thus began the use of IBM machinery for cryptological purposes. While in World War II the use of such machines was greatest in *cryptanalytic* activities, it should be pointed out that in 1935 the personnel of the Signal Intelligence Service were primarily interested in using the machines for *cryptographic* purposes. The machines eliminated the huge amount of drudgery attendant upon code compilation by hand methods, a task so great and tedious that it absorbed a disproportionately large portion of the time and energy of the entire SIS staff. With the IBM machines on hand, it was expected that most members of SIS would have more time to engage in cryptanalytic activities, for at this period the amazing possibility of using machine aids for cryptanalytic statistical work were as yet not recognized. This incident furnishes a good example of how a scientific development motivated by one need later becomes useful in providing for problems of a different need.

---

104. From July 1943 to September 1945 the Signal Intelligence Service was known as the Signal Security Agency. WGB

105. Date of note was 30 October 1934.

106. See Secret Supplement to the Annual Report of the Chief Signal Officer, 27 August 1935 (OCSigO 319.1), par. 2: *Revised Code Production Program,* 4 April 1935.

The IBM punched card system[107] employed perforated cards on which the contents of authorized codes were punched so that new editions could be prepared on short notice. Code manuscripts could be prepared by this method in much less time than was previously required by the older hand methods. Using IBM tabulating equipment the Signal Intelligence Service was able to complete a large code compilation program within a few months which otherwise would have required at least three years. A code that formerly required the services of four compilers for a period of six weeks to prepare could now be prepared in two days by a single operator. For example, the production of the Division Field Code required 136 man-hours of labor under the old method. The first new edition of the DFC produced using tabulating machines required only 50 man-hours, and subsequent editions required only eight man-hours. In addition, the machine method could be readily adapted to the reproduction of multiple copies by lithography, thereby eliminating the necessity of tedious proofreading.[108]

In general, the IBM method method of code production was considered from a practical viewpoint as "the most important development" that had ever taken place in cryptographic compilation.[109] It established a procedure for the efficient production of codes using minimum personnel. The problem of producing tactical codes in sufficient quantity for use during a war had thus been solved. Code production was streamlined to provide codes that would best serve the needs of the U.S. Army. The codes would be capable of serving rapid communications in conditions of mobile warfare; and very importantly it was felt that they would withstand attack against expert cryptanalysis. Not only was the code production program accelerated using tabulating machinery and hastened to completion before an actual emergency, but also improvements were devised for the adaption of the tabulating machines to other cryptologic uses. For example, a method of scrambling a set of ordered cards to produce a random arrangement of the data in the cards, invented by the Chief of the Signal Intelligence Service and one of his assistants, greatly increased the amount of time saved through the use of the machines.[110]

---

107. The IBM punched card system was the invention of Herman Hollerith (1860-1929), a mining engineer and statistician, who devised the system primarily to mechanize the counting of data. Its first big test came in 1890 when it was used with the U.S. census of that year. In many parts of the world, especially in England, IBM tabulating machines were known as Hollerith machines. Information was put onto cards by means of punched holes. Cards were then counted by using a series of wires that probed perforations as the cards passed by. Electrical circuits opened when holes appeared; otherwise electrical circuits were closed. WGB

108. See Secret Supplement to the Annual Report of the Chief Signal Officer, 27 August 1935 (OCSigO 319.1), par. 2: *Revised Code Production Program,* 4 April 1935.

109. This is of course before the era of the modern computer which has gone far beyond just replacing tabulating machinery. WGB

110. *Revised Code Production Program,* 4 April 1935.

CODE AND CIPHER COMPILATION 1930-1939

As a result of the revision of the code book production program and the transfer of the control of funds for printing and binding codes from The Adjutant General to the Chief Signal Officer, the amount of money now being directed to the Signal Intelligence Section for this work was greater than originally anticipated. The estimates, however, were never realized in the actual allotment of funds. Although it was understood that the War Department Budget Officer had approved $12,000 for this purpose for Fiscal Year 1935, the amount actually transferred to the Chief Signal Officer from the allotment of The Adjutant General was only $10,500.[111] By the autumn of 1934, the status of the code production program, as approved 22 March 1933, and revised by later changes in the system of secret and confidential cryptographic communications, was very different from that which had been originally devised.

War Department Staff Code No. 1 (WDSC-1) was printed in 1932 in an edition of 300 copies at a cost for printing and binding of $14,768.29. It was a two-part code in two volumes. Ten months were required for printing and binding this code, while its compilation in manuscript form had required the services of four cryptographers and two typists for over ten months. The entire edition was in secret storage.[112]

Military Intelligence Code No. 9 (MI-9) was printed in 1919 in an edition of 208 copies at a cost of $11,001.59.[113] Used for secret messages, it was a two-part code, of which five copies had been variously issued to military attachés in London, Paris, Berlin, Rome, and Tokyo. According to the Military Attaché in Tokyo, his copy had been destroyed[114] in the earthquake and fire of 1923, and the other four were recalled in 1930. In 1932 the title page of *Military Intelligence Code No. 9* (MI-9) was changed to read *War Department Staff Code No. 2* (WDSC-2). Later, in June 1938, at a cost of $231.44, a supplement to the code was prepared, covering new terms, names of persons and places, and types of equipment, to make the vocabulary current. The

---

111. Memorandum for The Adjutant General from the Executive Officer, OCSigO, Subject: *Printing and Binding Funds for Codes*, 17 July 1934 (SPSIS 111).

112. Memorandum for Major John H. Lindt from Major S.B. Akin, 24 September 1934 (SPSIS 111); Memorandum to Assistant Chief of Staff, G-2, from Executive Officer, OCSigO, 27 February 1933 (SPSIS 111).

113. See *The History of Codes and Ciphers in the United States During the Period Between the World Wars, Part I. 1919-1929*, pp. 9, 17, 41, 55.

114. Because the destruction of the copy could not be completely proven, the edition was withdrawn and held in reserve until a replacement (WDSC-3) could be prepared and printed.

entire edition was placed in secret storage in the Office of the Chief Signal Officer, as an emergency reserve for WDSC-1 until WDSC-3 could be printed.[115]

The old *Military Intelligence Code No. 5* (MI-5)[116] of which an edition of 800 copies had been printed in 1918 at a cost of $7,169.83, was still used by corps area and department commanders and military attachés in War Department communications. It also served for the exchange of military intelligence. The Adjutant General had destroyed 121 copies as unserviceable and 600 copies were still in storage in 1934. The edition was then revised for conversion into *War Department Confidential Code No. 1* (WDCC-1) and provided with a new title page and supplement. Outstanding copies were recalled and the new cipher device (Type M-138[117]) was issued for cryptographing secret messages between corps area and department commanders and the War Department. It was planned that when WDSC-3 and WDSC-4 were printed, the first distribution of WDCC-1 would be made. WDCC-1 had been authorized under the revised plan for the distribution of codes and ciphers. The converted code was designed for use with a cipher system then being devised. The cipher system operated by means of frequently-changed key words, which could be issued in the form of a single sheet at quarterly or semiannual periods.[118]

Military Intelligence Code No. 10 (MI-10), printed in 1927 in an edition of 120 copies at a cost of $3,000, was another secret, two-part code. The entire edition was in storage awaiting distribution when a revised plan was effected. *Military Intelligence Code No. 11* (MI-11) had been printed in 1933 at a cost of $1,474.12 for 200 copies. It was stored as the first reserve edition. In 1934 *Military Intelligence Code No. 12* (MI-12) was in the process of being printed and delivery was expected by the end of January 1935.[119]

All three editions of the Army Field Code (AFC) were nearly completed. AFC-1 had been compiles in 1925, but was not printed until 1932, at a cost of $3,382.92. Both AFC-2 and AFC-3 were in the press in 1934. AFC-2 was to be delivered by the middle of December 1934, while delivery of AFC-3 was expected by 1 March 1935.[120]

---

115. Memorandum for Major John H. Lindt from Major S.B. Akin, 24 September 1934; Inclosure: Revised Code Production Program, par. 1.

116. See *The History of Codes and Ciphers in the United States During the Period Between the World Wars, Part I. 1919-1929*, pp. 6-9, 17-19.

117. The Cipher Device M-138 was also known as the "Strip-Cipher Device", a cryptographic duplication of the Cipher Device M-94. WGB

118. Memorandum for Major John H. Lindt from Major S.B. Akin, 24 September 1934; Inclosure: Revised Code Production Program, par. 6.

119. *Ibid.* par. 2b.

120. *Ibid.* par. 2b.

The Philippine editions of the *Division Field Code* (DFC) were incomplete in 1934. The edition of DFC-5, printed in 1922 at a cost of $940.52, was compromised ten years later, when the loss of one copy in the Ninth Corps Area was discovered. All outstanding copies were then recalled and the edition was stored for use in special exercises or joint maneuvers. The reserve edition (DFC-9) was then distributed. It had been printed in 1926 at a cost of $1,116.68. All but 270 or the 2,070 copies printed were issued to the Philippine Department, to the Hawaiian Department, to United States Army troops in China, and to the Ninth Corps Area. DFC-11, printed in an edition of 2,000 copies in 1933, at a cost of $806.78, became the first reserve edition in storage. The second reserve edition (DFC-13) was scheduled for production in Fiscal Year 1935 and was completed and printed in that year. The number of reserve editions required by current war plans was then complete.[121]

The three editions of the *Division Field Code* destined for use in the Hawaiian Department had also been completed. DFC-6, printed in an edition of 2,000 copies at a cost of $776.43 in 1922, had been distributed to users. DFC-10 was printed in 1926, in an edition of 2,000 copies at a cost of $1,301.03. It was a reserve edition in secret storage. The second reserve edition, DFC-12, was completed in 1933 at a cost of $947.06.[122]

Two of the continental editions of the *Division Field Code* had been printed. DFC-7, printed in an edition of 5,000 copies in 1923 at a cost of $1,227.33, had been distributed to the communication centers in the Panama Canal Department and the Eighth Corps Area. Some 4,950 copies of DFC-7 remained in storage. DFC-8, of which 5,000 copies were printed in 1924 at a cost of $1,250, likewise was in secret storage. In accordance with the production schedule, DFC-14 was published in Fiscal Year 1935.[123]

The *Air-Ground Liaison Code* (AGL) was another authorized code whose production was expedited. AGL-2, printed in 1930 in a confidential edition of 14,000 copies at a cost of $136.85, had been partially distributed for training purposes, but some 6,500 copies were still in storage. This code and *Fire Control Code No. 2* (FC-2) were printed on the obverse and reverse sides of the same sheet of cardboard. Under the revised plan, these codes were printed independently. AGL-2 had been authorized as a confidential code and was subject to frequent change, thereby

121. *Ibid*, par. 6.
122. *Ibid*. par. 7.
123. *Ibid*. par 8.

demanding new editions. FC-2, on the other hand, had been revised and improved in 1931. It was for Official Use Only and its contents were standardized. Four editions of the AGL Code were scheduled for publication in Fiscal Year 1935. It was decided, however, to prepare only one new edition of the AGL Code, because of the pressure of other work and the desirability of testing a new vocabulary before printing the reserve editions.[124]

An Air Corps Command and Liaison Code was considered necessary for use by aircraft engaged in distant reconnaissance and tactical missions. Though it had not yet been officially approved for use, it was listed in the tentative Cryptographic Security Manual. Four editions of this code were scheduled, but preparation was not authorized.[125]

Two editions of the *General Address and Signature Code,* authorized several years earlier, had been produced. They worked satisfactorily enough, reducing telegraphic expenses considerably, but when the War Department, in the interests of governmental economy, extended its telegraphic services to other departments, the code proved to be unsuited for this type of traffic. As a result, the *General Address and Signature Code* was abandoned by 1934. Looking back, this was a step in the wrong direction, for security in time of war is greatly enhanced by such a code.[126]

The *Radio Service Code* had first been prepared and published in 1922, in a confidential edition of 7,000 copies at a cost of $1,550.[127] Of this edition, some 1,600 copies were distributed for training. By 1934 the code was not considered worthwhile and it was recommended that it be revised or recalled.[128]

The old *War Department Telegraph Code 1919*[129] was still in service but was no longer used for secret messages. Some 600 copies had been issued to the various posts and stations, and additional copies were distributed as required.[130]

---

124. *Ibid.* par. 9.

125. *Ibid.* par. 10.

126. See *The History of Codes and Ciphers in the United States During the Period Between the World Wars, Part I. 1919-1929,* pp. 23-24.

127. *Ibid.* p. 25.

128. Memorandum for Major John H. Lindt from Major S.B. Akin, 24 September 1934; Inclosure: Revised Code Production Program, par. 14-16.

129. See *The History of Codes and Ciphers in the United States During the Period Between the World Wars, Part I. 1919-1929,* pp. 13-16.

130. Memorandum for Major John H. Lindt from Major S.B. Akin, 24 September 1934; Inclosure: Revised Code Production Program, par. 14.

Meanwhile, the necessity to have available a publication that contained the most important data relative to authorized codes and ciphers had been recognized. In 1931 the Military Intelligence Division had prepared such a manuscript, but before funds for its printing could be appropriated, it had been necessary to make certain important changes in the system of codes and ciphers used within the Army. Therefore, a revision in the manuscript became necessary. Finally, the project was authorized in 1932 and undertaken toward the close of Fiscal Year 1933.[131] By 1934 a tentative edition of the *Cryptographic Security Manual* (CSM-1) had been distributed to all holders of secret codes.[132]

The purpose of the *Cryptographic Security Manual* was to give information essential to the protection and proper handling of secret and confidential codes and ciphers.

The increased international tension in the latter part of the decade and the corresponding necessity for concluding the Army's code production program in time to meet any emergency were factors that caused an increase in code and cipher printing and binding estimates after 1934. The estimate for printing and binding codes for the Fiscal Year 1935 was $20,618 and that for the succeeding year rose to $30,000. Yet the printing of WDSC-3 and WDSC-4 had to be postponed because in reality the funds allotted for 1936 amounted to only $8,700. The original edition of that code had cost $14,768.29 in 1932 and it was estimated that each of the two volumes required for the remaining two would cost $9,000.[133] By 1935 it was evident that the reason for the failure to adhere to the approved code production program was the fact that sufficient funds to cover the annual requirements under the program had never actually been made available. Consequently, shortages had to be made up in succeeding fiscal years.[134]

From year to year codes scheduled to be printed were postponed. Estimates were made, allotments were cut, codes were rescheduled. In 1935 it was estimated that $21,400 would be required in Fiscal Year 1937 and in succeeding years $35,050 would be sufficient to complete the program.[135] In 1937 only the sum of $17,400 was made available. A reduced estimate of $19,600 with a balance of $10,450 was required to complete the program. The sum available in 1938 was $15,000, a reduction from the $16,400 allotted. By 1939 the estimate was $24,600 with which it was proposed to print all remaining codes except WDSC-4. By this time the rapid

---

131. Supplement to the Chief Signal Officer's Annual Report, 1933, pp. 7-8.
132. Revised Code Production Program, 4 April 1935, par. 16.
133. Estimate for Printing and Binding, Fiscal Year 1936, 18 September 1934 (SPSIS 111).
134. Revised Code Production Program, 4 April 1935.
135. Memorandum for Colonel Stanley from Major H.L.P. King, 18 October 1935 (SPSIS 111).

progress made on the Converter M-134 indicated that it would serve the purposes for which WDSC-4 was intended, and that production of that code might be deferred.[136]

The publication of authorized codes was not the only item in the estimates for printing and binding and their preparation was not the only cryptographic burden on the personnel of the Signal Intelligence Service. In addition to authorized codes, which expanded in number as the world situation became more critical, cipher keys, cipher alphabets, and pamphlets of instructions for the codes, cipher systems, and cipher devices had to be prepared, published, and distributed.

SECRET ARMY–NAVY INTERCOMMUNICATIONS

The only means for secret intercommunication between the Army and Navy in joint exercises in 1943 was the old *Army-Navy Cipher No. 1,* the multigraph edition of which had been distributed in 1925.[137] This cipher was unsuitable for heavy traffic.[138] In 1931 in collaboration with the Code and Signal Section of the Navy, a cipher system had been developed for use between the two services. It was a system using the Cipher Device M- 94, which was recommended by the Joint Board as a substitute for the code book which had been authorized and compiled but never printed.[139]

It was concluded that a cipher device was better for joint intercommunications than a code, and experiments were initiated by both the Army and the Navy to develop a more practical and secure device than the M-94. An improved model of the Cipher Device M-94 was constructed and tested to determine its adaptability. It was found to be superior to the old one, although further modifications were still desirable for increasing its speed of operation.[140] After the development of the M-138, it was substituted for the M-94.[141]

Cooperation between the two services also included joint experiments with aircraft codes. An experimental edition of an aircraft code, *Tentative Aircraft Code No. 1,*

---

136. Estimates for Funds for Code Production for the Fiscal Year 1939, 27 July 1937 (SPSIS 111).

137. See *The History of Codes and Ciphers in the United States During the Period Between the World Wars, Part I. 1919-1929,* pp. 32, 36.

138. Revised Code Production Program, 4 April 1935, (SPSIS 311.5), par. 4.

139. Supplemental Report to the Annual Report of the Chief Signal Officer, Fiscal Year 1931 (SPSIS 319.1), p. 2.

140. Supplement to the Annual Report of the Chief of the Signal Officer, Fiscal Year 1933, Codes and Ciphers, (SPSIS 319.1), p. 8.

141. Supplement to the Annual Report of the Chief Signal Officer, Fiscal Year 1936, 31 August 1936 (OCSigO 319.1), p. 21.

for use in joint Army-Navy operations was authorized in 1933 by the Joint Board. It was prepared in an edition of 500 copies at a cost of $89.15 using Signal Corps funds. It was distributed by the Signal School to certain headquarters where joint exercises were conducted at frequent intervals. After service tests, necessary modifications were made in a second edition.[142] An equivalent code, *Tentative Aircraft Signal Book No. 4,* was produced and issued by the Navy. Both codes were used side by side to determine their relative merits.[143]

THE DEVELOPMENT OF CRYPTOGRAPHIC MACHINERY

One of the activities of the Code and Cipher Section, Office of the Chief Signal Officer, as has been related,[144] concerned the development of automatic cryptographic machinery. After 1930 experimentation in the development of cryptographic machinery was continued by the Signal Intelligence Service and work was also done on the improvement of hand-operated cipher devices.

Cipher Device M-94 had been used extensively since 1923 and an improved model was produced in 1931. As originally developed, Cipher Device M-94 was based on cryptographic principles worked out by Colonel Parker Hitt[145] which had been adapted to practical use by research work conducted by Lieutenant Colonel Joseph O. Mauborgne when he was Chief of the Engineering and Research Division, Office of the Chief Signal Officer, during World War I. Essentially, the device consisted of a series of disks fastened together on a central shaft, with the possibility of rearranging the order of the disks at will. On the circumference of disks were stamped mixed cipher alphabets. In the model as originally adopted, the disks were made of metal and the alphabets could not be changed without manufacturing new disks. In an improved model an attempt was made to paste strips of paper on the circumference, so that the cipher alphabets might be changed more readily.

A new device, Type M-138, was developed, procured in limited quantity, thoroughly tested, and finally approved for use in 1935. It employed changeable paper-strip alphabets, which for the purpose of encipherment were inserted in channels on a metal base. Attempts were made to get the Aluminum Company of America to manu-

---

142. Supplement to the Annual Report, Fiscal Year 1933, p. 7; *Revised Code Production Program,* 4 April 1935, par. 13.

143. *Revised Code Production Program*, par. 13.

144. See *The History of Codes and Ciphers in the United States During the Period Between the World Wars, Part I. 1919-1929,* p. 31.

145. See *The History of Codes and Ciphers in the United States During the Period Between the World Wars, Part I. 1919-1929,* p. 19.

facture these devices but they were unable to do so. In the end, Price Brothers, a small firm in Frederick, Maryland, was induced to attempt to make the devices, which they succeeded in doing using laminated bakelite.[146] The first thirty of these devices were manufactured at a cost of $15 each and delivered in April 1935. The security of the device was very high,[147] since the cipher alphabets could be changed in relation to the volume of the traffic. An instruction pamphlet was issued to all holders and the system was placed in operation on 1 July 1935. This device was also employed by the Navy.[148]

By 1938 a new cipher device, Type M-161, was being developed to provide a small machine for use in combat operations. It was, however, never put into production; and, instead, the M-209 (Hagelin) machine was substituted for it before the outbreak of war. The first mention of the development of the M-161 in the files is contained in a statement by Major S.B. Akin:[149]

> It is of the greatest importance that early efforts be devoted to the production of a means of rapidly encoding, cryptographing and decryptographing messages for:
>
> Aviation
>
> Mechanized units
>
> Front line (infantry-artillery liaison) units.
>
> Has the field been fully explored for a rapid mechanized means of the required size and weight? I consider this far more important at this time than machines for the use of rear elements ...[150]

To this, Mr. Friedman replied in a first indorsement: "We have nothing but Cipher Device M-94 and Air-Ground Liaison Code No. 2." The next item in the file is a memorandum from Major Henry L.P. King to Mr. Friedman, dated 28 September 1935:

> Please let me have a written report on the status of the device for cryptographing and decryptographing messages for aviation, mechanized units and front line units that Col. Akin directed you to devise in his April 24th memo.

The reply (30 September 1935) was as follows:

> At the time of my 1st indorsement to Col. Akin's memo of April 24, I had in mind a small device which, however, did not produce a written record. I understand that a device which does not produce a written record will not be considered, because of the impracticability of having to write down by hand the results of the operation of the device.

---

146. Later, the Aluminum Company of America did manufacture metallic boards.

147. Actually, the cryptographic security of the M-94, and its successor, the M-138, was not very high. Indeed, we know now that it was one U.S. cipher system that both the Japanese and the Germans were able to attack, sometimes with success. WGB

148. Secret Supplement to the Annual Report, Fiscal Year 1935, par. 3.

149. Memorandum from Major S.B. Akin to William F. Friedman, 24 April 1935.

150. Do front line, low echelon units really need cipher machines to cryptograph and decryptograph "traffic" of an operational nature? Simple codes, frequently changed, might better offer the degree of security and practicality needed when speed, rather than security, may be most important. WGB

I think this case should be considered as a phase of the project recently set up under title Converter Type No. M-161.

By Oct. 5 I expect to hand in draft specifications and drawings covering a modified Converter Type M-134-T2[151] which will[152] become the basis of Converter Type 161. It can readily be used as a basis for discussion with R&D with Labs.

Action 3 of the paper just quoted (by Major King, 1 October 1935) asked the question: "Will the device mentioned in paragraph 3 above meet the military characteristics of the M-161?" Action 4 gives the reply:

One form of the device will meet the military characteristics of M-161. The cryptographic principle is such that a machine for large fixed installations is merely an extension of parts of a basic assembly. The principal difference between a machine for small, mobile stations (M-161) and one for large, fixed stations (M-134-T3) lies in the printing or recording mechanism. For the M-161 we must have a very small, simple device not necessarily a page printer. For the M-134-T3 we must have a large, sturdy, electrically operated typewriter like the electromatic. The small printer must be worked out, and I have what I think are practical ideas along this line.[153]

Action 5 (Major King to Mr. Friedman, 1 October 1935) is as follows:

Please note second paragraph of Col. Akin's basic memo — all work in a modification of the M-134-T2 must be suspended if the work interferes with the development of the M-161. I consider the development of the M-161 to be the most important project now before your section.

Action 6 dated 3 October 1935 and signed by Mr. Friedman is as follows:

There is *nothing* about what I am now working on in connection with project of Converter M-161 which will in any way interfere with the projection of the two M-134-T2 models. And I absolutely concur with your statement that the development of the M-161 is *the* most important project before my section at the present time. I am pushing this as fast as possible and am most anxious that a start be made. I would like very much to talk the various designs over with the LABS, and am going to hand in draft specifications and drawings by October 5 for your action.

The military characteristics of the proposed cipher machine, to which the nomenclature of M-161 had been given, were set up as follows:

1. This machine should be designed for the fundamental purpose of enciphering and deciphering messages with speed, accuracy, and security equal to that of the present Division Field Code or better.

2. It should consist of a single unit, combining a 26-element keyboard and an indicating device making a printed or written record, either in tape or page form.

---

151. The M-134-T2, a five-rotor cipher machine, about which more will be said later, with certain modifications became the Army's very secure and still classified cipher machine, the Converter M-134-C (SIGABA). WGB

152. Several years later (27 January 1938) Mr. Friedman added a note in the margin: "It did not, however."

153. See footnote 152. Mr. Friedman (27 January 1938) added another note in the margin: "This describes a machine which did *not* become the M-161 but is now assigned the No. SISDE-11." A more recent note underneath (3 August 1944) says: "Became M-134-C SIGABA."

3. The weight of the machine including its carrying case should not exceed 15 pounds. It should be rugged in construction, capable of withstanding the jarring incident to its being carried and used in the vehicles for which intended.

4. The apparatus should be mechanically operated so far as possible, but electrical circuits for effecting the cryptographic substitution are admissible. The record may be made by mechanical, electrical or chemical agencies not requiring the use of carrying of liquids for development.

5. The minimum speed of operation in enciphering and recording or deciphering and recording should be approximately 60 characters per minute; the optimum speed would be 150 characters per minute.

6. The device should be operated in any position and should require the services of a single operator for maximum operating speed. The operation should be simple enough so that an average enlisted man can be trained to operate the device efficiently after one day's instruction.

These were forwarded to the Signal Corps Laboratories by Lieutenant Colonel Roger B. Colton for the Acting Chief Signal Officer on 10 September 1935. Although a letter of Major W.S. Rumbough to the Research and Development Division dated 8 November 1935 stated that the Secretary of War had approved the military characteristics and that the papers were being forwarded to the Signal Corps Laboratories for study and comment, the papers were not actually forwarded until 6 April 1936,[154] and before that date the sum of $250 had been allotted to the Laboratories for preliminary work on the M-161 and the design submitted by Mr. Friedman was being studied by the Patent Section.[155]

The development of the M-161 was now in the hands of the Signal Corps Laboratories and following the military characteristics of the proposed cipher machine work was progressing there but along what lines the Signal Intelligence Service did not know. The following quotation is from a routing and work sheet dated 10 September 1936 from William F. Friedman to the Chief, War Plans and Training Division:

1. In connection with development of automatic cipher machinery, about 1-1/2 years have gone by since this section submitted sketches of a machine which offers *great* possibilities not only for fixed station message centers but also for small, mobile units. This case has been assigned the type number M-161. Funds were established in current budget for its development but I do not think anything has yet been done on it.

2. Is it possible that this development could be let by contract to a commercial firm like Westinghouse or General Electric? In this connection I would like to point out that the Navy has given up trying to develop apparatus of this kind at their labs or shops and are committed to a policy of outside development.

---

154. According to a marginal note by Mr. Friedman.

155. See First Indorsement, 22 January 1936, Chief, Research and Development Division to Chief Signal Officer, basic letter of Major Rumbough to the Research and Development Division, asking what action concerning the M-161 had been taken.

Action 3 on this was as follows:

> Comments of the Signal Corps Laboratories are attached. It appears there is little if anything to gain by farming out this development, even if funds were available, and they are not without discharging a portion of the staff.

Nearly a year later, the Signal Intelligence Service still had not learned much about the work being done on developing the M-161 in the Signal Corps Laboratories.[156]

> In connection with the development of the Converter Type M-161 it is understood that this project has been assigned B priority and that work has been initiated and is progressing on same in the Signal Corps Laboratory. Informal attempts on our part to ascertain the lines upon which the development is based have been unsuccessful. It is believed highly desirable that the Signal Intelligence Section be given an opportunity to examine the proposed scheme and basic cryptographic principle before any further work is done on the project; otherwise it may develop that considerable time and effort will be wasted.[157]

William F. Friedman's communication, above, to the War Plans and Training Division stimulated a letter to Lieutenant Colonel William R. Blair at the Signal Corps Laboratories dated 30 July 1937, signed by Lieutenant Colonel Louis B. Bender, as follows:

> The War Plans and Training Division[158] is getting a little concerned about the progress of Project 104 and without any cooperation on their part. If I am correctly informed, you are pursuing on this project a somewhat different plan than was originally intended. That fact does not appear from the reports to date, but it is my impression that I was so informed on some visit to the laboratory. I believe that the original plan contemplated some sort of electrical mechanism, for which you have since found what you think is an acceptable mechanical solution. I should like to be set straight on this subject in some detail.
>
> I fear this project may become a bone of contention between the laboratory and the War Plans and Training Division. Naturally, they feel that they have all the available knowledge on the subject of ciphers and cipher machines. That being the case they feel that advantage should be taken of their experience and knowledge of this subject. On the other hand, you probably feel that you should be free to use any design that appears to be most suitable to obtain the objectives that the War Plans and Training Division may set up.

Colonel Blair at the Signal Corps Laboratories replied on 3 August 1937 as follows:

> I regret that the War Plans and Training Division is concerned about the progress of project 6-a on Converter M-161 and do not understand why they should feel that their ideas and suggestions are not being given consideration at the Laboratories. The idea that we are pursuing this project in a different manner than was originally intended is erroneous.

---

156. From a routing and work sheet from W.F. Friedman to the War Plans and Training Division, 15 July 1937.

157. Of course the Signal Intelligence Section was anxious to see the "proposed scheme" of the M-161 which the Signal Corps Laboratories, on their own and without formal cryptographic knowledge, was developing. WGB

158. That is, by the Signal Intelligence Service which was part of the War Plans and Training Division.

The military characteristics for the Converter M-161 are contained in a letter from OCSigO to The Adjutant General dated October 22, 1935, file OCSigO 413.52 (M-161) subject "Military Characteristics for Converter, Type M-161" from which is quoted par. 1*d* as follows: "The apparatus should be mechanically operated so far as is possible but electrical circuits for effecting the cryptographic substitution are admissible. The record may be made by mechanical, electrical or chemical agencies not requiring the use of carrying of liquids for development."[159]

The 2nd indorsement to the above-mentioned letter from the OCSigO to Director, Signal Corps Laboratories, dated November 13, 1935, file OCSigO 413.52 (M-161) 10-22-35, contained the following instructions. "Your preliminary investigations of this project will be conducted with a view to arriving at a solution by the use of a strictly mechanical device or devices and without the aid of any electrical features."

The investigation directed by the 2nd indorsement mentioned above resulted in the conception of several mechanical solutions. These ideas were not sufficiently developed at the time Mr. Friedman last visited these Laboratories to justify discussion and presentation. It was felt that a number of details should be proved in drawing layouts and in construction form prior to discussion.[160]

Work on the construction of the first service-test model has been intermittent due to personnel being required for work on projects of higher priority. Active work on project 6-*a* was not started until completion of the Converter M-134-C. In this connection, see 1st indorsement, OCSigO to Director, Signal Corps Laboratories, dated July 14, 1936, file OCSigO-111-FY 1937 (7-8-36). Work on the Converter M-134-C was not completed until June 1, 1937.[161]

A preliminary proposal for a converter M-161 dated April 6, 1935, was submitted by Messrs. Friedman and Rowlett by letter from OCSigO to Director, Signal Corps Laboratories, dated April 6, 1936, subject "Inventions of Cryptographic Mechanisms — Messrs. Friedman and Rowlett" with the statement "This is for your information, file and such use as you may care to make of it. Acknowledgement of receipt by indorsement is desired." The device described is the practical counterpart of the Converter M-134 without the tape transmitter but substituting therefor control commutators. This proposal was given consideration [with respect to the development of the M-161] but was not deemed a mechanical solution as outlined in the military characteristics and directive contained in second indorsement of November 13, 1935, mentioned above.[162]

The drawings for the building of the first service-test model of the Converter M-161 are about 75% complete. Some construction work of minor parts for the service-test model has been completed and it is the plan of these Laboratories to have the first service-test model completed for service test about April 1938.

---

159. It appears that the six characteristics shown on pages 41-42 are paragraphs 1*a* to 1*f* in the OCSigO letter quoted. WGB

160. It is difficult to imagine how the Signal Corps Laboratories, who had virtually no knowledge of cryptography, were permitted to construct a cipher machine (the M-161) before discussing its principles with the experts in the Signal Intelligence Section, War Plans and Training Division. WGB

161. On the other hand, the Signal Corps Laboratories did an outstanding job in completing the M-134-C, the highly secure SIGABA cipher machine widely used by the U.S. for high-level secret communications during World War II. But here the Signal Corps Laboratories followed the "principles" and guidance provided by the Signal Intelligence Section. WGB

162. It appears that the Signal Intelligence Section made a cryptographically acceptable proposal to the Signal Corps Laboratories, but it was turned down on the grounds of not being a mechanical solution. WGB

> We would be pleased to have Major Rumbough, Mr. Friedman or any other representative of the War Plans and Training Division visit the Laboratories and acquaint themselves with the drawings and layouts and the progress which has been made on their development to date. It must be understood, of course, that our development work is definitely guided and limited by the project not falling within the military characteristics set up or that does not come to us as a directive or an authorized modification of the military characteristics, while it may be helpful, may not properly be incorporated in the design.[163] In view of the work that has been done on this project in accord with present directive and the great probability that an entirely successful mechanical device will result,[164] I should regard a change in directive at this time as unfortunate indeed. It would not only delay the project but would set aside a large amount of good work that we could ill afford to waste in this way. However, if it appears wise to you to authorize a change in the military characteristics of this device, the sooner they are changed the better.

In accordance with the suggestion contained in the letter just quoted at length, Major Reeder and Mr. Friedman visited the Laboratories on 1 October 1937, and as a result of this visit, "two devices representative of the M-161" were to be sent to the Signal Intelligence Service.[165] Still, it was not until 29 April 1938, almost six months later, that the Director of the Signal Corps Laboratories wrote as follows:

> The construction of the subject machine [the M-161] has reached the stage where preliminary and improvised tests are feasible. In these tests it is found that the machine functions satisfactorily in the encipherment and decipherment of messages but that certain modifications and refinements are desirable..."[166]

Six weeks later, a second indorsement dated 13 June 1938 reported that a Converter M-161 and tape numbering machine were being delivered to the Office of the Chief Signal Officer. Three days later the Laboratories reported[167] that prior to that date a total of $10,025.90 had been spent on the development of the M-161 and that it was estimated that a model M-161-T-2 would require an additional $7,413 in the next fiscal year (1939).

Finally, a security study of the M-161 as developed by the Signal Corps Laboratories could now be made. It was assumed that the enemy had captured one of the machines and therefore knew of its construction.[168]

---

163. Meanwhile, the Signal Corps Laboratories relentlessly pursued their own development of the Converter M-161, oblivious to cryptographic security requirements, "guided and limited by the military characteristics set up." WGB

164. Of course an entirely successful mechanical device will result, but how secure will it be? WGB

165. Letter from Director, Signal Corps Laboratories, to the Chief Signal Officer, 7 October 1937.

166. Still overlooking the security aspects of the M-161, the Signal Corps Laboratories are highly pleased that "the machine functions satisfactorily in the encipherment and decipherment of messages." WGB

167. Director, Signal Corps Laboratories to Chief Signal Officer, 16 June 1938.

168. Quite correct. When evaluating any cryptographic system it must always be assumed that the "enemy" has full knowledge of all details concerning the general system. Only specific keys may be considered as "secret" or unknown factors. WGB

Two messages were prepared with indicators and texts unknown to the cryptanalysts who made the study.[169] The probable-word method was used as a point of attack. It was assumed that the word INFANTRY appeared in the messages. In the first message the word was not found, but in the second it was found in 30 minutes time. Having found the assumed word, the correct initial setting of the machine was determined in 15 minutes and the complete message was deciphered. Solution of the first message required approximately three hours, owing to the number of probable words tried. The story of the Signal Corps Laboratories' ill-fated cipher machine (the M-161) came to an end. The following words expressed it best: "The degree of security afforded by this machine is considerably less than that afforded by our present Cipher Device Type M-94."[170]

Even before the Signal Intelligence Section had made its security study of the M-161, negotiations had begun which ultimately led to the adoption, with modifications, of a cipher device invented by the Swedish inventor Boris Hagelin. Because it was believed that the Hagelin device might offer a better solution to the problem of providing secure communications for lower-echelon units than the one which had been developed by the Signal Corps Laboratories, the Laboratories were directed[171] on 17 August 1938 as follows:

> In view of that report [i.e. the security study] no further development work will be undertaken on this project pending results obtained with the Hagelin Cryptographer Type B-360, for which you are negotiating purchase. The funds remaining to the credit of this project after that purchase will be reallocated to other projects on your program following your recommendations on this subject.

Rights to the manufacture of the Hagelin Cryptograher Type B-360, to be known as the Cipher Device M-209, were therefore purchased from Boris Hagelin.

By the end of World War II many thousands of Cipher Device M-209 were being used by U.S. military forces as their primary low-echelon cryptographic system.[172]

---

169. More specifically one cryptanalyst, Frank Rowlett.

170. Letter of Lieutenant Colonel L.B. Bender to the Director, Signal Corps Laboratories, 12 July 1938, inclosing the Signal Intelligence Section's report concerning the M-161.

171. First indorsement to letter of 16 June 1938.

172. The demise of the M-161 was certainly well deserved. But as far as acquisition of the M-209 is concerned, in fairness to William F. Friedman—since the security afforded by the M-209 is also in question—it should be noted that he never enthusiastically supported purchase of the M-209. As Colonel Akin of the War Plans and Training Division put it, "We have to have something." WGB

CIPHER DEVICE M-209

The mechanical Cipher Device M-209, conceived by Boris Hagelin, was used by U.S. Forces in World War II as a field cipher machine for sending classified messages.

CIPHER MACHINE M-134-C (SIGABA)

The U.S. Army's cipher machine M-134-C was also known by its short-title, SIGABA. To the U.S. Navy this machine was known as the ECM Mark II.

EVOLUTION OF THE M-134-C (SIGABA)

Let us briefly now follow the evolution of the U.S. Army's secure and efficient cipher machine, the Converter M-134-C, also known by its short title, the SIGABA.

In January 1933 a model of an automatic cipher device (M-134-T1) was completed. In the M-134-T1 the stepping of one code wheel was irregular and under the control of a keying tape. In the M-134-T1 electric control of rotor or code wheel stepping made its first appearance.[173] Tests demonstrated that the M-134-T1[174] was reliable but certain limitations in the speed of its operation — it used only one rotor,[175] the keying element being external and supplied by a tape which could be fed into the machine as desired — indicated that further improvements were needed. The design was modified and submitted to the Signal Corps Laboratories for further development. The necessity for a new cipher machine had become extremely urgent, because the time required to encode and decode messages using the traditional codes had become a bottleneck in practically all headquarters.[176]

A new and more efficient automatic cipher machine (Type M-134-T2) was completed in May 1934. In the M-134-T2 there were five rotors, instead of one as in the M-134-T1. As in the M-134-T1 an external tape was used for supplying the keying element. Designed to be connected directly to an electric typewriter,[177] the M-134-T2 was capable of attaining a speed of from 30 to 40 words per minute during encipherment and decipherment. This speed was much more rapid than that of the previous M-134-T1

---

173. If the "key" on the keying tape was random and unpredictable, the M-134-T1 was similar to a completely secure one-time tape system. WGB

174. On 25 July 1933 the Chief Signal Officer filed a patent application (Serial No. 682,096) on behalf of the inventor, Mr. William F. Friedman.

175. In the M-134-T1, as letters were enciphered, its single rotor would step through a number of positions, depending upon the specific "key" on the keying tape. The result was that encipherment, letter by letter, was slow. WGB

176. Supplement to the Annual Report of the Chief Signal Officer, Fiscal Year 1935, par. 1h, p. 8; Annual Report of the Signal Intelligence Section, Fiscal Year 1935, par. 1.

177. Electric typewriters earlier had been used as "printing mechanisms" for several cipher machines in Europe. They contained solenoids for each key. During the enciphering (or deciphering) process, an electric current, after passing through the maze of a succession of rotors, would traverse a tubular coil of wire, thereby causing a particular solenoid to become magnetized and to allow its key to strike the platen of the typewriter. WGB

and far more rapid than that which could be achieved using a code book. Moreover, the cryptographic principle of the M-134-T2 provided the highest degree of security.[178]

Steps were taken to place a contract for these converters[179] with the firm of Wallace and Tiernan, Belleville, New Jersey, a small manufacturing company. About 15 June 1935, before delivery of the first machines from Wallace and Tiernan, Mr. Frank B. Rowlett, then principal assistant to Mr. Friedman, conceived an idea which later would become the basis for the particularly high degree of security afforded by the M-134-C (SIGABA).[180]

Convinced of the soundness of the idea proposed by his assistant, Mr. Friedman proceeded to draft specifications and drawings covering a modified Converter Type M-134-T2, the new cipher machine to be known as Converter Type M-134-T3.[181] To convince others of the great value of Rowlett's idea, especially the Signal Corps Laboratories, was not an easy task. The story of the Signal Corps Laboratories' singular attempt to build the ill-fated cipher machine M-161 has already been told. Neither funds nor time were available at the Signal Corps Laboratories to turn from their design for the M-161 to Friedman's proposed M-134-T3. Even worse, the Director of the Signal Corps Laboratories was keeping their design of the M-161 under close wraps, even from the Signal Intelligence Section, and wished to make no changes in the design, despite urgent recommendations by Mr. Friedman that he do so. The Chief Signal Officer took the position that in view of the approaching emergency, it was better to be supplied with actual machines of somewhat inferior design than to have no machines at all.[182]

At this point let us turn briefly to the contributions, especially as they concern cipher machines, of Edward H. Hebern. He was the inventor, at least in the United States, of the first cipher machine that employed rotors.[183] Hebern spend his life

---

178. Annual Report of the Signal Intelligence Section, Fiscal Year 1934, par. 1c; Supplement to the Annual Report, Fiscal Year 1935, pp. 10-11.

179. M-134-T2 cipher machines. WGB

180. The course of military cryptography in the United States was changed by Frank B. Rowlett's idea. Instead of dependency upon slow and clumsy codes, the U.S. now had available a secure and rapid means of communication. Without Rowlett's idea, events of World War II might have been different. What would the scenario of World War II have been if the enemy had been able to read the secret communications of the U.S., just as the U.S. was able to read German and Japanese secret communications? In October 1964 Frank B. Rowlett received a very well-deserved Congressional award of $100,000 for his idea. WGB

181. See Footnote 153. The M-134-T3 later became the Converter M-134-C (SIGABA). WGB

182. See Footnote 172. As it turned out, the M-161 was of such inferior design that it was worthless. WGB

183. See U.S. Patent 1,683,072: Edward H. Hebern's "Electric Code Machine."

FRANK B. ROWLETT

Colonel Frank B. Rowlett was one of the original three principal assistants to William F. Friedman in the Signal Intelligence Service. He was Chief, General Cryptanalytic Branch, Signal Security Agency, from 1943 to 1945 when he became Chief, Intelligence Division, later the Operations Division, Army Security Agency. In May, 1946 he reverted to inactive duty. Cryptographically he is particularly noted for his important contribution in making the M-134-C (SIGABA) secure against cryptanalytic attack. Cryptanalytically he is noted for guiding U.S. efforts in breaking the Japanese Purple Machine.

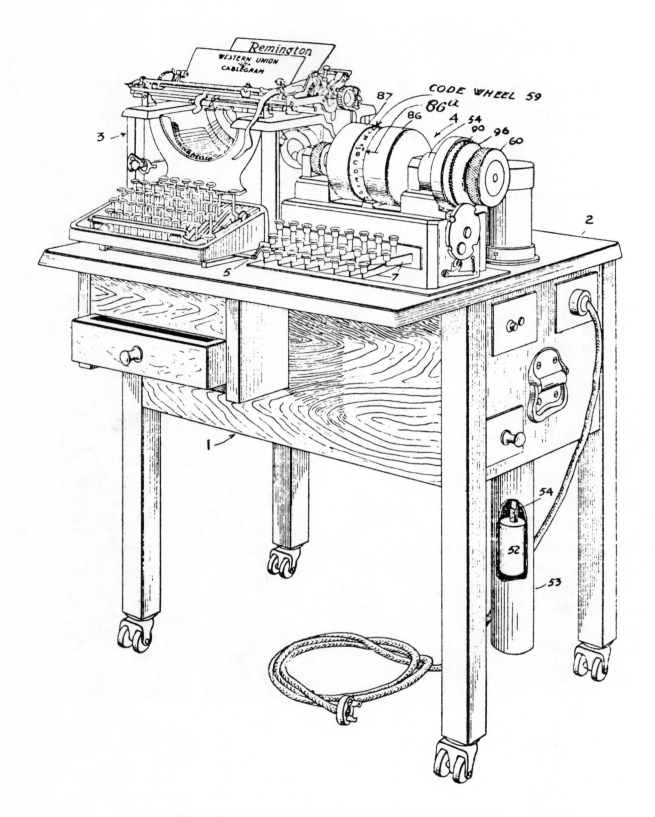

HEBERN'S ELECTRIC CODING MACHINE

Edward H. Hebern's Electric Coding Machine as illustrated in his Patent 1,510,441 of September 30, 1924. Note the single code wheel and mechanical typewriter.

attempting to have his machines accepted as a means of providing secure communications. Although his first machines attracted considerable interest he was successful in selling only a limited number of cipher machines in the 1920s and early 1930s. Unfortunately, his cipher machines never received the acceptance which he wished. Perhaps we shall never know the real influence that Hebern's machines had on the already discussed development of cipher machines by the Army's Signal Intelligence Service. We do know that Mr. Friedman was aware of Hebern's early rotor-type cipher machines and he had a measure of success at solving ciphertext messages produced by what he termed mechanico-electrical cryptographs.[184]

The Navy had taken great interest in Hebern's machines. In 1931 they purchased some 30 machines which they termed Mark I machines. By 1934, however, William F. Friedman had demonstrated to the Code and Signal Section of the Navy that the Hebern machines were insecure.[185]

Shortly after this, in October 1935, Lieutenant J.N. Wenger, USN, of the Code and Signal Section of the Navy, approached the Signal Intelligence Service with a request for assistance in designing the cryptographic principles of a new machine, the Navy being then dissatisfied with the degree of security afforded by their Mark I machine. With approval of his superiors, Mr. Friedman revealed[186] the principles of the Rowlett-Friedman invention to the Navy, but at that time these principles were apparently[187] not of particular interest to the Navy.

Soon, however, Naval officials took more than just a casual interest in the Rowlett-Friedman invention. They already were using a number of previously purchased Hebern machines to handle a considerable amount of Navy traffic, and the ease of using a cipher machine's keyboard to encipher and decipher messages was appreciated. Whereas the Army lacked funds for cryptographic development, being already committed to the M-161, the Navy seemingly had funds available[188] for the development and procurement of new cipher machinery.

---

184. *Analysis of a Mechanico-Electrical Cryptograph, Part I* (1934). Prepared by William F. Friedman; *Analysis of a Mechanico Electrical Cryptograph, Part II* (1935). Prepared by William F. Friedman on the basis of tests conducted in 1932.

185. *Ibid.*

186. These revelations to various Naval officers were made on three occasions: 23 October, 31 October, and 1 November, 1935.

187. According to a document by Captain L.F. Safford, USN, one of the officers who later became acquainted with the record of the Rowlett-Friedman invention, this was true at that time.

188. One unsubstantiated rumor was that the Navy had $1,000,000 available. WGB

Led by Captain Laurence F. Safford, USN, a dedicated and skilled Naval cryptologist, the Navy took an important step.[189] They began the task of building a cipher machine, or ECM as they termed it. Moreover, it was decided that the ECM would contain the vital principle of the Rowlett-Friedman invention.

Having digressed to briefly outline the story of how the Navy came to build a cipher machine cryptographically equivalent to that proposed by William F. Friedman,[190] let us return to the continuation of the story of the Army's procurement of the M-134-T2 cipher machines, now termed M-134-A machines, at the point where we left off: the placing of a contract for these converters with the firm of Wallace and Tiernan.

By 1937 a few of the M-134-A machines had been completed. Two were placed in the Signal Intelligence Service and to were taken by Mr. Friedman to Panama. Service tests were made and the fact established that the machines were successful. When more machines had been completed, additional installations could be made. By mid-1938 Wallace and Tiernan had delivered more machines. Accordingly, the Quartermaster General was requested to ship seven Converters M-134-A in the strong room of the United States Army Transport *Republic* on 15 November 1938. Two were to be delivered in Panama, one in San Francisco and four in Honolulu. Two of the latter would later be shipped to Manila by the United States Army Transport *Grant* on 6 March 1939.[191] Mr. Friedman accompanied these converters as far as Honolulu. In Panama, San Francisco, and Honolulu, he set up the converters and tested them.

A surprise awaited Mr. Friedman when he returned to Washington. The Navy had completed construction of a prototype model of its new ECM and Friedman and his key assistants in the Signal Intelligence Service were invited to view the new machine.

The Navy's ECM was a success in every way. It provided the highest degree of cryptographic security and, it did not require external tapes to be used for supplying the keying element.

In 1939 Germany invaded Poland and much of Europe was at war. For the United States, World War II was clearly on the horizon. The Navy received delivery of their new ECM's. The Army continued to use the M-134-A, although inconvenienced

---

189. Without the probable knowledge of William F. Friedman or the Signal Intelligence Service. WGB

190. The M-134-T3. WGB

191. Letter, Chief Signal Officer to the Quartermaster General, Subject: Shipment of Converters M-134, 10 October 1938 (SPSIS 320.3).

by the need for external keying tapes. It was not until Pearl Harbor and the entry of the United States into World War II that the Army and Navy seriously combined their efforts with respect to cryptographic systems. The need for joint systems was critical. Early in 1942 the Navy transferred to the Army a number of ECM's which were designated the M-134-C by the Army and given the short title SIGABA.

The M-134-C shortly replaced the relatively few M-134-A machines previously set up by Mr. Friedman.[192] With mobilization now in full swing as American forces prepared for war in Europe and the Far East, the procurement of the Navy's ECM for use by both the Army and Navy began in earnest. Soon the M-134-C (ECM) was being used for secret communications throughout the military forces. Cryptologic experts of both services were convinced that the machine offered the highest degree of security. By the end of the war their confidence had been proven.

REVISION OF CRYPTOGRAPHIC PLANS 1938–1939

As the possibility of a general European war became more imminent, the Signal Intelligence Service carefully reexamined its means of cryptographic communications in order that the best methods might be available in the event of war.

It was found that the secret systems were too few and not distributed widely enough. Since secret means of communication could not be extended to a great number of holders, lest the entire system be jeopardized through increased traffic and the greater possibility of error, it was necessary to prepare more secret systems and give at least one of them a wider distribution.[193]

There was only one confidential system. The inevitable increase in traffic that could be expected after the outbreak of war would enhance the possibility of an enemy breaking the system. A compromise occurring at a single station would also involve the confidential communications at all stations to which the system had been issued. It was decided therefore to increase the number of confidential systems.[194]

The majority of all systems were still too slow. Electrical communications had become so rapid that any means of cryptographing and decryptographing that did not

---

192. The Converter Type M-134-A (M-134-T2) was used in the Philippines even after the Japanese invasion. A Signal Corps Radio Intelligence unit used the M-134-A to send certain high-priority intercepted Japanese messages back to the Signal Intelligence Service in Washington. Traffic and final "Good-byes" were sent up until Corregidor fell. WGB

193. Memorandum for The Adjutant General from the Chief Signal Officer, Subject: *Codes*, 28 April 1938 (SPSIS 311.5) par. 2a.

194. *Ibid.* par. 2.

afford a speed at least commensurate with that of the telegraph was too slow for practical purposes. Impatient commanders, unwilling to brook a delay, might direct that messages be sent in the clear, which would not only compromise their texts, but also might contribute to the solutions of other encrypted texts. The most immediate need was a more adequate means of cryptographing and decryptographing messages automatically. The cryptographic device M-138,[195] widely used and believed reasonably secure, was slow and cumbersome. Without the development of an automatic means of encipherment and decipherment it was believed that communications could not be both secret and meet the speed demanded by modern warfare.[196] The early adoption of a suitable field cipher device (M-161) was recommended.[197] Danger to cryptographic security lay in the fact that no centralized agency controlled security procedures. It was recommended that someone in each headquarters be designated as Cryptographic Security Officer with the duty of supervising secret and confidential communications, noting violations of regulations, etc.

Finally, it was concluded that sufficient new cryptographic systems should be authorized so as to prevent the accumulation of a large amount of traffic in any one system by foreign cryptanalytic bureaus. It was believed, however, that this could best be accomplished by the adoption of a relatively small number of basic cryptographic systems, variability being provided by the issuance of different keys to each group of users.[198]

For communication between the War Department and the corps areas, Cipher Device M-138 would be used until the Converter M-134 could be introduced with individualized keying procedures.[199] A similar secret system would be used between the War Department and the overseas departments and another between the War Department, corps areas, and overseas departments where more than one unit was concerned.[200]

Another secret system would be used between a larger group of holders including lower headquarters which at that time used the *Army Field Code* in unenciphered form. It was expected that the M-134 would be used in the future with individualized keying and the *Army Field Code* would be held in reserve. Messages to be repeated to

---

195. The so-called "strip cipher device." WGB

196. Memorandum for The Adjutant General from the Chief Signal Officer, Subject: *Codes,* 28 April 1938 (SPSIS 311.5) par. 2c.

197. *Ibid.* par. 2d.

198. *Ibid.,* par. 3.

199. M-134 with individualized keying procedures was the M-134-A (M-134-T2). WGB

200. Memorandum for The Adjutant General from the Chief Signal Officer, Subject: *Codes*, 28 April 1938 (SPSIS 311.5), Plans for codes, par. 1-3.

posts, forts, camps, arsenals, and depots would require a different system because the possibility of compromise was too great under the existing arrangement. The M-138 was recommended for this type of traffic. Although the M-138 was slow, the volume of traffic was not considered sufficiently large to necessitate a more elaborate device.[201]

It was planned to use the M-138 with the existing *Military Intelligence Code* and an individualized keying procedure for secret communications between the War Department and military attaches. Secret communications of the Military Intelligence Division and between the Army and Navy would continue to use the M-138. The double-transposition system would be used as an emergency secret system.[202]

For confidential communications, the Cipher Device M-161, then being developed, was recommended.[203] The M-94 would be used in such messages with the Navy and Coast Guard. No change was contemplated in the *Air Ground Liaison Code*. For restricted communications, the *War Department Telegraph Code* and *Fire Control Code* were still in use and no changes were contemplated.

CONCLUSION

Confronted with a restricted budget and the difficulty of assuming expanding responsibilities with limited personnel, the Signal Intelligence Service, building on the old code-production program, had by 1939 placed the development of military cryptography on a sure foundation.[204] The code-production program, in spite of revisions and postponements, was completed by the outbreak of World War II. Yet sufficient flexibility had been retained, and critical analysis of the program enabled the Service to adapt itself to the rapidly accelerating pace of military cryptography and its demands in an age of electrical communication. The security of the secret communications of the United States Army was well protected.

---

201. Memorandum for The Adjutant General from the Chief Signal Officer, Subject: *Codes,* 28 April 1938 (SPSIS 311.5), Plans for codes, par. 4, 6.

202. *Ibid.*, passim.

203. The Cipher Device M-161, developed by the Signal Corps Laboratories without the technical assistance of the Signal Intelligence Service, was never accepted. WGB

204. The Army's 1938-1939 cryptographic plans have been described. Available cryptographic systems included in 1939 the following —

    (1) Codes: Army Field Code
                  War Department Telegraph Code
                  Military Intelligence Code
                  Air Ground Liaison Code
                  Fire Control Code

The demands of secret traffic for General Headquarters of Armies and for divisions had likewise been satisfied. Each had the means of communication for warfare both within the continental United States and in the overseas departments. The demands for speed and accuracy in the intensity of modern, mobile warfare had also been anticipated. Tabulating equipment had reduced the length of time and the number of personnel required for the production of codes in the theaters of operation. Improvements in automatic cipher machinery through the introduction of electrical devices had made it possible to predict with confidence that cryptographic operations would not delay the transmission of important secret and confidential communications.

Indeed, the success of the Signal Intelligence Service appears not to have been unheralded abroad, despite the confidential nature of its work. In August 1935 the Code and Signal Section of the Navy and representatives of the Office of the Chief Signal Officer conferred on the matter of Japanese representatives who were visiting foreign countries to study cryptography and cryptanalysis. Their aim was to improve their own system of communications, stimulated no doubt by the revelations of Yardley's *The American Black Chamber*. Measures were undertaken to prevent the visitors from learning anything about the cipher machines made by Hebern.[205]

---

      (2) Cipher Devices: M-94

                                  M-138 (strip cipher device)

      (3) Double-Transposition cipher

      (4) M-134 with individualized keying procedures.

      (5) M-161 field cipher device, then being developed by the Signal Corps Laboratories.

In 1941 when World War II began for the United States, with the exception of the M-134-A, available Army cryptographic systems were *not* satisfactory. The 1938-1939 systems were slow and lacked the cryptographic security required. Fortunately for the Army, however, by 1941 the Navy had completed development of their own ECM (based on the Rowlett-Friedman invention). This important and secure cipher machine became the Army's M-134-C (SIGABA) and quickly became the workhorse of Army encryption methods for secret traffic. Of the army's cryptographic systems described as available in 1939, only the M-138 saw much use; and it was the one U.S. system that the "enemy" had some success at breaking. Later, in defense of the Signal Intelligence Service's cryptographic ability, they did develop several excellent systems, the M-228 (SIGCUM) and the SIGTOT (a one-time teletype tape system), to name two. But to say that the Signal Intelligence Service had by 1939 placed the development of military cryptography on a sure foundation, this Editor must disagree. WGB

205. See page 49 concerning Edward H. Hebern. Because of lack of funds in the Army, it was the Navy which took primary interest in Hebern's cipher machine. WGB

EARLY VERSION OF CIPHER DEVICE M-138

An early version of the U.S. Army's cipher device M-138, with carrying case, approximately 14" wide by 12" deep. Known as the strip cipher device, the M-138 cryptographically duplicated the Cipher Device M-94 which used aluminum wheels instead of paper strips. Later versions of the M-138 folded in the center for easy, compact carrying.

HERBERT O. YARDLEY

Herbert O. Yardley was Chief of the Cipher Bureau (MI-8), America's first code and cipher-breaking organization. After publication of his book The American Black Chamber *in 1931 he became persona non-grata to the U.S. intelligence community.*

CHAPTER III

SOLUTION AND TRAINING ACTIVITIES
1930 – 1939

THE TRAINING PROGRAM

One of the basic reasons for the transfer of solution activities from the Military Intelligence Division to the Signal Corps had been the desire to concentrate more effectively on the training of personnel in cryptanalytic work. It was, indeed, precisely in the sphere of training that Herbert O. Yardley's Cipher Bureau had been most deficient. The limited amount of training which had been carried on under the War Department auspices was the result of Signal Corps activity, not that of Yardley's Cipher Bureau.

The change in emphasis from solution of immediate value in the production of information also reflected the relatively lower interest which the War Department has in such information in time of peace. In the period 1919-1929, when the War Department had, with State Department support, maintained the Cipher Bureau, the chief value had been gained by the State Department, so that when the latter withdrew its support in 1929, the true level of interest in the War Department was revealed. The difficulties encountered in establishing facilities for adequate interception may have contributed to the result, though had this been the only factor, these difficulties could have undoubtedly been surmounted by the Signal Corps.[208]

As a matter of fact, the science of cryptography had been making rapid strides since 1919. The experiences of World War I had sharpened the interest of most governments in increasing the security of their communications, and the growing cryptographic maturity of the United States was probably only typical of what was taking place in most of the larger developed countries.

Moreover, American technological advances in the use of machinery and electricity during the War and in the first decade of the peace had made training which was adequate for the cryptographic tasks of 1918 wholly inadequate for those which were likely to be encountered in the case of another conflict.

---

206. See *The History of Codes and Ciphers in the United States During the Period Between the World Wars, Part I. 1919-1929*, pp. 160-162. Particularly note Footnote 400, p. 160. WGB

In addition, it was probable that after Yardley published *The American Black Chamber* in 1931,[207] even those governments which had hitherto been backward in the art would adopt new and better methods for preserving the security of their communications and developing for themselves their own cryptographic bureaus. Action by the Japanese Government was certainly to be expected, since in Yardley's book the solution of Japanese cryptographic systems was easily one of the most sensational disclosures.

Thus, it had now become imperative that an adequate force of cryptanalysts be trained for a future war. Since the training could not be obtained without contact with practical problems, it was out of the question for the Signal Intelligence Service to look for its specialists outside the War Department.

CRYPTANALYTIC TRAINING

The four young cryptanalysts who had been employed under Civil Service regulations in 1930, Frank B. Rowlett, Solomon Kullback, Abraham Sinkov, and John B. Hurt, began, under the tutelage of William F. Friedman, the Director of the Signal Intelligence Service, their extended training in various aspects of the work of the Signal Intelligence Service.[208] They gave early promise of ability and their progress in cryptanalysis was especially encouraging. By 1932 they were prepared to conduct research on their own in this field.[209]

The training which they received in cryptanalysis was at first largely theoretical, but many practical problems were supplied by the large number of cipher systems submitted by persons from many different parts of the United States and even from various foreign countries. Increased interest in cryptography had been aroused by the appearance in the public press of books and magazine articles dealing with cryptography and cryptanalysis.[210] Amateur cryptogram societies were organized[211] and syndicated cipher contests were conducted in various periodicals and daily newspapers.

---

207. For the story of Herbert O. Yardley and publication of his book, *The American Black Chamber*, see *The History of Codes and Ciphers in the United States During the Period Between the World Wars, Part I. 1919-1929*, pp. 133-160. WGB

208. One of them (Frank B. Rowlett) recalled in 1945 that owing to a severe shortage of space he was at first given a table in "the vault," a room in the Munitions Building in which existing stocks of reserve codes were stored.

209. Supplemental Report to the *Annual Report of the Chief Signal Officer, Fiscal Year 1931* (SPSIS 319.1), p. 5

210. A book has been published, *Solving Cipher Secrets* by M.E. Ohaver, which includes 73 weekly articles concerning cryptography and cryptanalysis, exactly as they appeared in the 1927-1928 weekly magazine FLYNN'S WEEKLY, later known as DETECTIVE FICTION WEEKLY. (Laguna Hills, CA: Aegean Park Press, 1982). WGB

211. The American Cryptogram Association still exists today. WGB

The Signal Intelligence Section examined all codes, ciphers, and cipher apparatus submitted to the War Department for consideration and possible adoption into the military service. Of the many submitted every year, only an extremely limited number (not over five) possessed sufficient merit even to warrant serious consideration for military use. In fact, the probability that persons outside the military service might invent cryptographic systems better than those actually in use became more than ever remote. The principal reason for this lay in the fact that the majority of the inventors had never had any experience in military cryptography and were not conscious of the many different requirements that had to be fulfilled by systems adapted to military usage. The invention of cryptographic systems became a profession in which only the highly skilled specialist could succeed.[212]

In the event of an emergency the Signal Intelligence Service would not be able to find, in civilian life, trained specialists in either cryptography or cryptanalysis in sufficient numbers to meet the requirements of the anticipated expansion. Consequently, it was necessary to conduct courses of instruction for carefully selected personnel who, as a result of the training, would be available for such duty in time of war.[213]

In recognition of the necessity for training some members of the Signal Intelligence Section in the Japanese language, a special course of instruction in Japanese was begun in September 1932. Mr. John B. Hurt, who was the Japanese expert of the section, taught this course until the end of April 1933, three hours per week being devoted to it. Mr. Hurt became ill in May and a competent civilian instructor had to be located to take his place.[214] A former colonel in the Imperial Russian Army, Mr. W. Ayvazoglou, now an American citizen, took charge of the course on 1 June 1933.[215]

THE SIGNAL INTELLIGENCE SCHOOL

In the 1930's the major portion of the training of a reservoir of qualified military personnel for cryptologic duties, for service in time of an emergency, was conducted through the Signal Intelligence School, attached to the Signal Intelligence Service and directed by Mr. William F. Friedman. The school grew out of provisions for the assign-

---

212. Supplemental Report to the *Annual Report of the Chief Signal Officer, Fiscal Year 1931* (SPSIS 319.1) p. 4; Data for Annual Report, War Plans and Training Division, 2 August 1932 (SPSIS 319.1).

213. Supplement to the Annual Report, 1933, p. 5.

214. Memorandum to the Assistant Chief of Staff, G-2, from the Executive Officer, Office of the Chief Signal Officer, 13 May 1933.

215. Memorandum to the Assistant Chief of Staff, G-2, from the Executive Officer, Office of the Chief Signal Officer, 20 May 1933.

ment of Regular Army officers to the Signal Intelligence Service, but before it was established a start had been made in the direction of training by the preparation of manuals.

Based on his earlier lectures on cryptography and cryptanalysis in the Signal School at Camp Vail[216] (after 1925 the Signal School was moved to Fort Monmouth, New Jersey), Mr. Friedman prepared training manuals in those subjects which by 1930 were used in connection with Army Extension Courses, offered primarily to reserve officers with a cryptological interest. For the first time in cryptological literature, Friedman's manuals presented the basic principles and methods of cryptography in a logically ordered form and represented pioneer work in cryptographic instruction. The texts prepared were *Elementary Military Cryptography* (1930)[217] and *Advanced Military Cryptography* (1931)[218] which became the standard treatises and were offered to the Army at large.[219]

In 1935 the Army Extension Courses were carefully revised to keep them abreast of the latest research in cryptology, and new problems were added. They were sent to The Adjutant General for publication and were proofread by the staff of the Signal School. Manuscripts of two special texts, covering the first two of an intended series of ten subcourses in cryptanalysis, were also written in 1935. They were designed to form the basis for lesson assignments in that subject and were, when published in 1938, the only texts of their kind. They were more complete and detailed than Mr. Friedman's previous monograph printed by the Government Printing Office in 1924, "Training Pamphlet No. 3," May 12, 1923, *Elements of Cryptanalysis*,[220] then used by the Army, Navy, and Coast Guard. The two manuscripts written by Mr. Friedman, but not published until 1938,[221] represented fifteen years of cumulated experience and research in cryptanalysis.[222]

---

216. See *The History of Codes and Ciphers in the United States During the Period Between the World Wars, Part I. 1919-1929*, p. 38.

217. Reprinted in 1976 by Aegean Park Press. WGB

218. Reprinted in 1976 by Aegean Park Press. WGB

219. Annual Report of the Chief Signal Officer, 1930; Supplemental Report to the Annual Report, 1931, p. 5.

220. *Elements of Cryptanalysis* was reprinted by Aegean Park Press in 1976. WGB

221. These two manuscripts, *Military Cryptanalysis, Part I* and *Military Cryptanalysis Part II* have been reprinted by Aegean Park Press. WGB

222. Signal Intelligence Section, Major Accomplishments, Fiscal Year 1935, par. 6. Between 1924 and 1943 Mr. Friedman prepared the following texts:
    1. *Elements of Cryptanalysis* (1924).
    2. *Elementary Military Cryptography* (1935, 1943).
    3. *Advanced Military Cryptography* (1935, 1943).
    4. *Military Cryptanalysis, Part I* (1938, 1942).
    5. *Military Cryptanalysis, Part II* (1938, 1941, 1943).
    6. *Military Cryptanalysis, Part III* (1939, 2nd ed., 1939).
    7. *Military Cryptanalysis, Part IV* (1941).

A second objective of the Signal Intelligence School's training program was to give junior officers in the Signal Corps actual instruction and experience in all phases of signal intelligence work. In addition to the two-week course for officers, which the Chief of the Signal Intelligence Section conducted at the Signal School, Fort Monmouth, New Jersey, a similar course in cryptography was conducted in 1929 for reserve officers in the Signal Intelligence School in the Office of the Chief Signal Officer. It was attended by 13 carefully selected Signal Reserve and Military Intelligence Reserve Officers and one special student assigned to the course by the U.S. Coast Guard.[223]

In the next year, authority was requested by the Chief Signal Officer to detail each year one specially selected junior Signal Corps officer as a student in the Signal Intelligence School. The request, approved by The Adjutant General on 11 October, was as follows:[224]

> 1. Reference is made to your letter of August 22, 1930, subject: Honor Courses in Service Schools [(A.G. 352.01) (8-18-30) Misc. (c)], in which, under Paragraph 6, there appears as one of the suggested study courses that of "codes and ciphers".
>
> 2. So far as this office is aware there is no civilian or military institution in this country at which special courses are conducted in the compilation, application, handling, or solution of military codes and ciphers. It is true that at certain of the service schools some instruction in code work is given, but this is very fragmentary and nowhere is there given adequate instruction in either compilation or solution of codes and ciphers. It is also true that from 1922 to 1929, inclusive, there was given annual at the Signal School, Fort Monmouth, a subcourse in Military Cryptography covering approximately twelve hours of lecture and classroom work and fifteen to thirty hours of home work, but this subcourse is no longer to be given. At best it could only cover some of the broad and more general features of code work but could not go into detail on account of the limited time available.
>
> 3. A recent change in Army Regulation (Change No. 1, AR 105-5 of May 10, 1929) assigns to the Chief Signal Officer very important responsibilities in connection with the solution of codes and ciphers and the preparation and detection of secret inks. As a result of this added responsibility there has recently been organized in this office a Signal Intelligence Service under which all work connected with secret communications is concentrated. Among these activities is that of instruction of military personnel and civilian personnel of the War Department in cryptography and allied subjects. Regular courses of instruction are to be conducted for Reserve Officers and certain of the Army Extension Courses are to be administered and conducted directly by this office. In order to accomplish this instruction efficiently, much time and labor has been expended in the preparation of training courses.

---

223. Annual Report, 2c(2), p. 6.

224. The Chief Signal Officer to The Adjutant General, Subject: *Detail of Officers for Instruction in Cryptography*, 2 October 1930 (AG 352.01, 10-2-30, Misc.; AGO, 10-4-30 to G-3). The letter was signed by Colonel G.E. Kumpe, Executive.

4.   While a certain amount of valuable instruction in these subjects can be conducted by the correspondence method, the time required to become at all proficient with the administrative and technical details of the operation of an efficient Signal Intelligence Service is far beyond that available to officers engaged in other work.   Moreover, much of the material is of such a nature that it does not lend itself to absorption by the correspondence method. It should also be recognized that the training of commissioned personnel for duty in this important service ought not be left a matter of individual inclination or idiosyncrasy. During time of war, sufficient experienced commissioned personnel at least to administer this service in an efficient manner, if not to engage in its technical control, will be unavailable unless a logical program for their instruction is established and conducted in the same manner as is the case with other military subjects.

5.   This office has given considerable thought to this matter and submits the following recommendations:

(1)   That one Signal Corps officer, not above grade of 1st Lieutenant, be detailed annually to this office for a full year's instruction in the compilation of codes and ciphers, the solution of codes and ciphers, the operation of radio intercept and radio goniometric organizations, and the preparation and detection of secret inks.

(2)   That the officer so detailed should not be considered as an addition to the quota of commissioned personnel assigned to the Office of the Chief Signal Officer, but solely as a student on the same basis as other officers attending institutions of learning in the capacity of students.   He should have no duties other than those connected with his studies.

(3)   That, if this project is approved, the first officers selected for this duty be chosen in time to commence instruction by June 1, 1931, the course to be completed by June 1, 1932.

First Lieutenant Mark Rhoads, Signal Corps, was the first officer to be so detailed.[225] He reported on 8 September 1931, for a year's training. Meanwhile, arrangements had been made for the assignment of First Lieutenant J.C. Sherr,[226] Signal Corps, as a language student in Japan for four years. Lieutenant Sherr sailed for Japan in August 1931 and after completing his studies returned to the Signal Intelligence School for cryptanalytic training.

By the end of Fiscal Year 1932, it was evident that one year was insufficient for the required instruction and authority was requested to extend the course to two years. The basic document is as follows:[227]

---

225. In 1935 Captain Rhoads was sent to the Philippines but soon afterwards contracted an illness which forced his retirement from the Army.   He ultimately recovered from this illness, but in spite of repeated requests for a return to active duty, both by Captain Rhoads and the Signal Intelligence Service, no change in status was permitted by the Surgeon General. In January 1944, however, Captain Rhoads became Assistant Director of Communications Research in the Signal Security Agency with the status of civilian employee.

226. Colonel Sherr served during the early part of the War in the Philippines but was killed in September 1943 as a result of an airplane accident while on temporary duty in India.

227. Acting Chief Signal Officer of the Army to The Adjutant General, Subject, *Detail of Signal Corps Officers for Instruction in Cryptography* (OCSigO 210.6 Gen), approved in 1st Indorsement, 29 April 1932 (AG 350.01, 23 April 1932, Misc. C.).

Reference is made to a letter dated October 2, 1930 from this office, subject as indicated above, and to your indorsement dated October 11, 1930, [A.G. 352-01 (10-2-30) Misc. C.] in which approval was granted for the establishment of a one-year course of instruction to be given at this office in the various phases of the work of the Signal Intelligence Service. In accordance with the aforementioned authority, 1st Lieut. Mark S. Rhoads, Signal Corps, was selected as the first student for this one-year detail and he began the course on September 6, 1931.

2. The above-mentioned officer has proved to be an apt student and this office considers his selection as having been thoroughly satisfactory. Despite a most consistent application to duty, however, it has become apparent that one year is hardly sufficient to cover the ground contemplated by this office when the course was projected and authority to establish it as a one-year course was requested. The seven months that have been spent by this student officer in the pursuit of the course have been devoted thus far only to a study of the various types of cipher systems, and these have by no means yet been covered in a manner considered adequate by this office. No time has been devoted to the analysis of any code systems, which represents a most important phase of modern military cryptography; neither has there been any time as yet for the study of radio intercept and goniometric operations, nor of the preparation, use and detection of secret inks. It is obvious that the failure to make a closer approximation of the time required to cover the ground is occasioned by the fact that this course has never been given before, and that no course even remotely similar to it is to be found at any civilian institution in this country.

3. It is estimated that at least two months' additional time should be devoted to the study of cipher machines; six months to the study of code systems; two months to the study of radio intercept and goniometric operations, and one month to the study of secret inks. Such a schedule would require the present student's continuation on this duty until about April 1, 1933, allowing for no leave of absence whatever. It is felt, however, that the nature of the work and the degree of concentration required are such that no officer should be expected to subject himself to this type of mental strain for more than nine consecutive months, without a rest period of at least one month. Hence, allowing for one month's leave, the present student could be expected to cover the ground intended by about May 1, 1933.

4. In view of the foregoing situation, this office requests authority to extend the present course until about May 1, 1933, and to establish it as a regular two-year course on the same basis as the two-year courses pursued by officers attending civilian institutions. The course should commence in September, should allow for one months leave of absence during the next summer, and then reopen to continue until about the following May.

5. In view of the short period of time now available for decision as to the subjects to which the remainder of the present student officer's time should be devoted, it is requested that action on the recommendations made in paragraph 4 be expedited. No additional funds are involved.

Lieutenant Rhoads was continued as a second year student in the school and a second student officer, First Lieutenant W. Preston Corderman, was selected as the first year student.[228] It was proposed that upon the completion of his second year, Lieutenant

---

228. Colonel W. Preston Corderman served as Chief, Signal Security Agency, and as Commanding Officer, Second Signal Service Battalion, from 1 February 1943 to 31 March 1946. For much of this period he was also Chief, Signal Security Branch, Office of the Chief Signal Officer, and Commanding Officer, Arlington Hall Station, and he held the temporary grade of Brigadier General from 18 June 1945 to 31 March 1946.

Rhoads would be replaced by another student. Thus, there were always two officers pursuing this special course, one in his first year, and the other a second year student.

The experience of Lieutenant Rhoads in his two years of training reflected the variety of training in all aspects of signal intelligence work which was offered in the school at that time. He spent seven months on 61 cipher problems, six months on code problems, four months in the study of cipher machines, three and a half months in code compilation and administrative problems, and two weeks on secret inks. During his second year, he studied Japanese with Mr. Hurt for three hours a week for eight months and took and elementary course in Russian at the Department of Agriculture for two hours a week for eight months.[229]

In addition to the two Signal Corps officers trained in the Signal Intelligence School, reserve officers also attended the school between 1929 and 1933. During this period Signal Reserve Officers, Military Intelligence Reserve Officers, and one Coast Guard Officer were ordered to active duty for a period of two weeks. The number in attendance each year was as follows:

Year	Signal Reserve	Military Intelligence Reserve	United States Coast Guard
1929	5	5	1
1930	8	8	
1931		No funds available	
1932	3	2	
1933	3	2	

The number of personnel completing the Extension Subcourses from 1931 to 1933 was as follows:

Year	Sig. C.	Sig. Res.	Nat. Guard	M.I. Res.	Other
1931	2	3	–	–	–
1932	3	6	1	–	–
1933	2	15	–	2	4

Until the summer of 1934 instruction in cryptology was conducted by civilian personnel of the Signal Intelligence Section, in addition to other duties, but by November 1933, it was already considered desirable for more of their time to be devoted to current research activities. The assignment of a Regular Army officer as

---

229. The Chief Signal Officer from First Lieutenant Mark Rhoads, Subject: *Report Covering Course in Codes and Ciphers,* 28 July 1933 (SPSIS-201 Mark Rhoads).

an instructor was requested for this reason and because it would permit the expansion of the extension and resident courses. Finally it was hoped that the assignment of Regular Army personnel would render the Signal Intelligence Service less dependent on civilian personnel.[230] In July 1934, a Regular Army Officer (First Lieutenant W. Preston Corderman) was detailed as instructor and the school was formally organized as a separate and distinct unit. War Department restrictions limited the number of officers assigned to duty in Washington and only one officer was detailed as a student in the Fiscal Year 1935, and it was recommended that an increase in the number of student officers be authorized.[231] In 1935 the number was increased to two, in addition to the instructor, but appointments were to be made every two years, instead of annually as before, so that the average number of officers per year was still only one. This move made it possible to give identical courses to both officers, instead of a first-year course to one and a second-year course to the other.[232]

The material studied by the students of the Signal Intelligence School from 1934 to 1936 included formal courses, special lectures and conferences, and visits of inspection. The schedule of courses was as follows:

4 September 1934 to 4 April 1935: Analysis of cipher problems, with special emphasis on the applications of mathematics to cryptanalysis.

5 April 1935 to December 1935: Analysis of code problems, consisting of both one-part and two-part codes with superencipherment. The security of the Division Field Code was studied. Some familiarity with the adaptation of International Business Machines to code problems was imparted.

2 January 1936 to 29 February 1936: Analysis of cipher devices and mechanisms, including the Wheatstone Device, the M-94, the Kryha Machine, and the IT&T Machine.

Two courses were given in the Japanese language.

15 March 1935 to 30 June 1935: Two hours per week.

1 September 1935 to 29 February 1936: Six hours per week.

Dr. Abraham Sinkov, Dr. Solomon Kullback and Lieutenant Mark Rhoads expanded the curriculum with lectures on the application of mathematics to the

---

230. Memorandum for Major John B. Wogan, G-2, 4 November 1933 (SPSIS 353.16).

231. Secret Supplement to the Annual Report, 1935, Sec. III, Par. 1.

232. Supplement to the Annual Report, 1936, p. 22; The Adjutant General to the Chief Signal Officer, Subject: *Quota of Students at the Cryptographic and Signal Intelligence School*, 8 October 1935 (SPSIS 352).

solution of transposition ciphers (nine lectures); permutation tables (three lectures); statistical methods in cryptanalysis (16 lectures); and the work of the Provisional Radio Intelligence Detachment,[233] 1933-1934 (one lecture). Visits of inspection were made to the Accounting Division, Public Works Agency, to witness the operation of business machinery, 9 November 1934, and the United States Coast Guard Monitoring Station, Fort Hunt, Virginia, on 16 November 1934.

In this period First Lieutenant W. Preston Corderman served as Instructor and First Lieutenant Harrod G. Miller,[234] Signal Corps, and Lieutenant (j.g.) Leonard T. Jones, USCG, were the regular students. In addition, Captain Edward J. Vogel[235] and First Lieutenant Ulrich S. Lyons[236] of the Military Intelligence Reserve, and Captain J.B. Mathews,[237] Captain Ware, and Captain Cooper of the Signal Reserve received instruction in the analysis of cipher problems during their two-week tours of active duty in May and August. Three other persons, two staff-sergeants, and Mr. Pickering, of the Department of Justice, received instruction in cryptography.[238]

Some of the students were exchanged with the Federal Bureau of Investigation, which afforded Signal Intelligence personnel facilities and instruction in document examination. In return FBI personnel received instruction in cryptography and cryptanalysis. This cooperation was found to be mutually advantageous.

The question of the removal of the Signal Intelligence School from Washington to Fort Monmouth was considered first in 1934. The school, located in Washington, was not a part of the Office of the Chief Signal Officer, but rather an activity conducted under his supervision, "because of the impracticability of providing elsewhere adequate facilities in the way of secret material and qualified personnel."[239] Hence, it was considered advisable, in 1934, that the Signal Intelligence School should be kept in Washington "until actual, working signal intelligence units" were established elsewhere.[240]

---

233. On this topic, see below.

234. Colonel Miller served in Europe during World War II.

235. Captain (afterwards Major) Edward J. Vogel was, from 1943 to 1945, Officer in Charge of the Special Examination Unit, Signal Security Agency, except for a period of detached duty in the European Theater.

236. Captain Lyons (afterward Major) served in the Signal Security Agency in 1942 and 1943.

237. Lieutenant Colonel J.B. Mathews was Administrative Officer at Arlington Hall Station until 1 February 1943.

238. Signal Intelligence School during period September 4, 1934-February 29, 1936 (SPSIS 352).

239. Memorandum for the Chief of Staff from Brigadier General Alfred T. Smith, Subject: *Cryptographic and Signal Intelligence School,* 11 September 1933 (SPSIS 352).

240. Memorandum on Signal Intelligence School, 23 February 1934 (SPSIS 352).

Following the establishment of a signal intelligence detachment at Fort Monmouth however, the question of moving the school to Fort Monmouth appeared no more feasible.   It was considered to be functioning satisfactorily at that time in the Office of the Chief Signal Officer, and its removal would be detrimental to the training of the students and instructor,[241] but the plan of the Chief Signal Officer to augment the Signal Intelligence School made it necessary finally to remove it to Fort Monmouth, where it could also train enlisted personnel.   Therefore, on 7 September 1939 The Adjutant General approved its transfer from Washington, effective during the Fiscal Year 1941.[242]   The training of officers was retained in Washington as a responsibility of the Signal Intelligence Service.   The list of officers in the Signal Intelligence School is as follows:

The Signal Intelligence School
Officers in Attendance[243]

Dates	Students	Instructors
Sept. 1931 — June 1933	First Lieutenant Mark Rhoads	W.F. Friedman
June 1932 — June 1934	First Lieutenant W. Preston Corderman	W.F. Friedman
Sept. 1934 — June 1936	First Lieutenant Harrod G. Miller Lieutenant Leonard T. Jones	First Lieutenant W. Preston Corderman
Aug. 1936 — June 1938	First Lieutenant George A. Bicher First Lieutenant Charles B. Brown	Captain H.G. Miller
Aug. 1938 — June 1940	First Lieutenant J.C. Sherr First Lieutenant H.G. Hayes	Captain G.A. Bicher
Aug. 1940 — 7 Dec. 1941	Captain Harold Doud First Lieutenant E.F. Cook Lieutenant Rhoads, USCG	Captain H.G. Hayes

---

241. Memorandum for the Chief Signal Officer from Major W.S. Rumbough, Subject: *Location of the Signal Intelligence School,* 6 February 1936 (SPSIS 352).

242. The Adjutant General to the Chief Signal Officer, Subject: *Signal Intelligence Service,* 7 September 1939 (SPSIS 352).

243. This list is based on material in SPSIS 201, and SPSIS 352.16.

THE ARMY AMATEUR RADIO SYSTEM

Since 1935 the Office of the Chief Signal Officer had conducted training of and maintained close connections with the American Radio Relay League. In 1924 the Signal Corps School recommended that the members of this leading organization of amateurs should be affiliated with the Army. The plan was approved 28 September 1925 and a net control station was set up at Fort Monmouth in charge of an Army liaison officer. An amateur in each Corps area was to initiate the plan, organize a net, and keep records of its activities. Many members resigned after the initial enthusiasm had diminished, but the plan was revived in January 1929. The Army net control station was moved to Washington. The Army Amateur Radio System rendered valuable assistance in relief in disasters, cooperating with the American Red Cross. Starting with a small membership, the number of those interested increased steadily until, in 1939, there were 1,700 members.[244]

This organization also proved its value in experimental work and tests, under the War Plans and Training Division. News of these activities was reported in the *Signal Corps Bulletin* and *QST*, the organ of the American Radio Relay League. Instruction in the use of codes and ciphers was added to the training aspect of this program in 1930. This had a decided value as a war time training measure and increased the interest of the Army amateurs in their avocation. A special cipher system was prepared for use by the amateurs in conducting regular communications. The venture was so successful that further training along these lines gave early promise of becoming an important part of the regular activities.[245] Some of the amateurs were enrolled in the extension courses and demonstrated considerable ability in cryptanalysis. A greater number were issued "Cipher Busters" certificates for solving cryptograms during the Fiscal Year 1937.[246] Captain Norman L. Baldwin, who had taken practically all of the cryptanalytic course in addition to his regular duties while stationed in the Office of the Chief Signal Officer in 1931-1934, was in charge of this work.

---

244. Courtney R. Hall, *Development of the Office of the Chief Signal Officer,* Part 1, 1917-1943. (Control Approved Symbol SPSEO-100, Project D-1. Historical Section Field Office, Special Activities Branch, Office Service Division, Office of the Chief Signal Officer), p. 22.

245. Annual Report, 1930.

246. Colonel Stanley L. James to Chief Signal Officer, Subject: *Army Amateur Cryptanalysts,* 24 February 1938 (SPSIS 311.5).

CRYPTANALYTIC RESEARCH AND SOLUTION

When the civilian cryptanalysts became sufficiently expert in the subject, special research in cryptanalytic theory and procedure was conducted. The results obtained were embodied in classified technical papers for reference purposes and for the training of personnel. Some of these papers represented important advances in the application of complex statistical methods. Procedures were devised for the solution of the difficult double transposition cipher and for the scientific construction of permutation tables for code compilation.[247]

Studies were also made of various codes devised by the Code Compilation unit to determine the degree of their security. In one investigation it was concluded that the addresses and signatures of tactical messages should either be omitted or by cryptographed by a system other than that used for the text of the messages. Steps were taken to eliminate this threat to cryptographic security.[248]

By 1935 a series of technical papers on cryptography and cryptanalysis had been published for a restricted distribution.[249] The manuscripts were edited and a number written by the Chief of the SIS.

The series was as follows:

a. *Analysis of a Mechanico-Electrical Cryptograph*, Part 1 (1934). Prepared by William F. Friedman.

b. *General Solution of ADFGVX Cipher* (1934). Based on *Elements of Cryptanalysis,* Signal Corps Training Pamphlet No. 3 and a paper by First Lieutenant J. Rives Childs, *Report on German Military Ciphers*.

c. *Permutation Tables Involving a Feature of Non-Transposability* (1934). Prepared by Dr. Abraham Sinkov.

d. *Existence of Alphabets Having No Internal Repetitions* (1934).

e. *Permutation Tables for the Most Important Commercial Codes* (1934).

f. *Principles of Solution of Cryptograms Produced by the I.T.&T. Cipher Machine* (1934). Based on the solution of messages of the model installed in the Department of State, 1931.

---

247. Supplement to the Annual Report, 1933, p. 8; Annual Report, 1933, p. 8.
248. Annual Report, 1934, par. 2.
249. Signal Intelligence Section, Major Accomplishments, 1935, par. 5.

g. *German Military Ciphers from February to November 1918* (1935). Based on report of First Lieutenant J. Rives Childs, prepared in 1918.

h. *The Principles of Indirect Symmetry of Position in Secondary Alphabets and their Application in the Solution of Polyalphabetical Substitution Ciphers* (1935). Prepared by William F. Friedman.

i. *The Index of Coincidence and Its Application in Cryptanalysis* (1935). Prepared by W.F. Friedman.

j. *Field Codes Used by the German Army during the World War* (1935). Prepared by W.F. Friedman.

k. *Statistical Methods in Cryptanalysis* (1935). Prepared by Dr. Solomon Kullback.

l. *Principles of Solution of Military Field Codes Used by the German Army in 1917* (1935). Based on a brochure by a British Officer of the Code Solving Section, General Headquarters, British Expeditionary Force, 1919.

m. *Course in Cryptography Translated from the French Work of General Givierge* (1934). Translated by John B. Hurt.

n. *Notes on the Liaison Service and the Liaison Intelligence Service of the German Army during the World War* (1935). Based on a report of Captain Philip B. Whitehead, F.A., prepared in 1919.

o. *Analysis of a Mechanico-Electrical Cryptograph*, Part II (1935). Prepared by W. F. Friedman on the basis of tests conducted in 1932.

p. *Report of Code Compilation Section, General Headquarters, American Expeditionary Forces* (1935). Prepared by Captain Howard R. Barnes, SigC, in March 1919.

q. *Final Report of the Radio Intelligence Section, General Staff, General Headquarters, American Expeditionary Forces.* Prepared by Lieutenant Colonel Frank Moorman, General Staff Corps.

r. *The Contribution of the Cryptographic Bureaus in the World War* (1935). Prepared by Yves Gylden and reprinted from the *Signal Corps Bulletin*, 1933-1934.

s. *Further Application of the Principles of Indirect Symmetry of Position in Secondary Alphabets* (1935). Prepared by Frank B. Rowlett, based on work begun by William F. Friedman in 1923.

In the next quadrennium four other papers were added to this list:

a. *Studies in German Diplomatic Codes Employed During the World War* (1937). Prepared by Dr. Charles J. Mendelsohn, formerly Captain, Military Intelligence Division, General Staff, based on work in Washington (1918-1919).

b. *An Encipherment of the German Diplomatic Code 7500* (1938). Prepared by Dr. Charles J. Mendelsohn.

c. *The Zimmerman Telegram of January 16, 1917 and its Cryptographic Background* (1938). Prepared by William F. Friedman and Dr. Charles J. Mendelsohn.

d. *Statistical Methods in Cryptanalysis* (revised, 1938). Prepared by Dr. Solomon Kullback.

In addition to the service rendered other governmental agencies in the construction of special codes and ciphers adapted to their needs, assistance was also given them in the solution of many code and cipher messages and in testing cipher machines which they were considering for adoption. In 1930, for three months, all of the personnel of the Signal Intelligence Section collaborated with the Code and Signal Section of the Navy Department in an attempt to solve certain Russian code cablegrams. These had been passed between the Amtorg Trading Corporation in New York and to headquarters in Moscow, and had been submitted by the Chairman of the House Committee engaged in the investigation of Communist propaganda in the United States. The Naval unit had already devoted three months to the study, without success, before the assistance of the Signal Intelligence Section was requested.

There was a similar lack of success in the joint efforts. Not a single code telegram in the Russian language, passing between officials of the Foreign Office of the Soviet Union, had been solved at this time. On the basis of authentic information, the code and cipher systems employed by the Imperial Russian Government were considered among the most complicated and effective in the world. The Soviet Regime had inherited and improved on these methods. It was considered doubtful, in 1931, whether any of these code telegrams could be read with the information available.[250] Later it was learned that these messages were all sent by the "one-time pad" encipherments of code groups taken from a large code. For this type of encipherment, properly prepared and properly used by cryptographic personnel, no general solution is as yet known (1945).[251]

---

250. Supplemental Report to Annual Report, 1931, pp. 6-7.
251. Nor will it ever be known. WGB

In 1932 another project was undertaken at the request of the Navy Department. For seven years the Code and Signal Section of the Navy had been engaged in the development of a cipher machine which it was hoped could be adopted for use throughout the service. The device had been designed by personnel of the Code and Signal Section in collaboration with personnel at the Navy Yard in Washington and a civilian inventor of long experience in the field, Mr. Edward Hebern. The naval experts were considerably impressed with the security of their device and challenged the Army to solve a set of test messages. The machine was furnished and keying instructions but not with the key list (daily settings) itself. The cipher texts of 55 messages were also furnished, together with their corresponding plain texts. In addition, the cipher texts of 110 other messages, all of the same cryptographic period as the 55 above-mentioned messages, were furnished, but without the plain texts. The Signal Intelligence Service personnel were challenged, even with all the foregoing material in their possession, to produce the solution to any one of the 110 cipher messages. In other words, it was intended that the experts in the Signal Intelligence Service would be presented with conditions even better than those usually present in attempting to solve the intercepted traffic of a single day's operations. This suggests that the Naval experts were extremely confident in the security of their new machine, for they permitted the test to be made under unusually favorable conditions.

The Signal Intelligence Service experts were successful in meeting this challenge. The indicator system was solved and a number of these messages read.[252] As a result of this test, the Navy continued to experiment with its machine in order to improve it.

A second project was also undertaken in 1932 at the request of the State Department. A highly complicated but well-built printing-telegraph cipher machine had been developed by Colonel Parker Hitt, a retired Army officer who for many years had been regarded as one of the leading experts in the field of cryptography and cryptanalysis.[253] The machines had been produced by the International Telephone and Telegraph Corporation and installed in the State Department for a test. The Secretary of State, not having any cryptanalytic staff, officially requested the Secretary of War to make suitable cryptanalytic studies to ascertain the cryptographic efficiency of the new machine. In order to provide material for the studies, ten cipher messages enciphered by the machine with settings not indicated were provided. The messages were solved in some cases after only thirty minutes' work and it was concluded that

---

252. See *Analysis of a Mechanico-Electrical Cryptograph*, Part II (1935), p. 7, for the details.

253. On Colonel Hitt's undeniable contributions to the science of cryptology in this early period, see the index to this and the preceding volumes.

practically any of the messages enciphered by the machine could be solved within a few hours. The insecurity of the machine was thus adequately demonstrated. It was also obvious to the International Telephone and Telegraph Corporation that the machine was not secure and further work on it was abandoned.

The cryptanalytic skill of the Signal Intelligence Service was put to another test in 1935. The German inventor, Kryha, had constructed a cipher machine which had been officially adopted by several governments. Abroad it had been heralded as absolutely indecipherable and was brought to the attention of the Chief Signal Officer in February 1935 by an American firm which had purchased the American rights to the machine for a considerable sum of money. After some correspondence, a test message was submitted by the purchaser as a challenge of the accuracy of certain contentions made by the Signal Intelligence Service. Solution was accomplished by a team of three cryptanalysts in little more than one hour and was in the mail within three hours of the receipt of the cryptogram. The method of solution was embodied in a technical paper.[254]

Considerable assistance was also given to the Department of Agriculture in 1932, in supplying the Crop Reporting Board with a set of code words with three-letter differences for telegraphic accuracy. The Department of Commerce was given cooperation in the solution of commercial messages referred to it by business houses. Continuous aid was given to the Coast Guard, Treasury Department, in the solution of difficult cryptograms.[255]

INTERCEPT ACTIVITY 1929–1939

The Radio Act of 1927, in its regulation of radio communications in the United States through the Federal Radio Commission, effectively outlawed the interception or divulging of information relating to the contents of messages. In 1934, when the Federal Communications Commission was created and assumed the functions of the Federal Radio Commission, the new legislation which was enacted did not relax the rigid prohibition of intercept activity. The Communications Act of 1934 contained the following provision:

---

254. *Revised Code Production Program*, Individual Mention of Machines, par. b; Supplement to the Annual Report, 1933.
255. Annual Report, 1932, p. 9.

Unauthorized publication or use of Communications

No person receiving or assisting in receiving, or transmitting, or assisting in transmitting, any interstate or foreign communication by wire or radio shall divulge or publish the existence, contents, substance, purport, effect, or meaning thereof, except through authorized channels of transmission or reception, to any person other than the addressee, his agent, or attorney, or to a person employed or authorized to forward such communication to its destination, or to proper accounting or distributing officers of the various communicating centers over which the communication may be passed, or to the master of a ship under whom he is serving, or in response to a subpoena issued by a court of competent jurisdiction, or on demand of other lawful authority; and no person not being authorized by the sender shall intercept any communication and divulge or publish the existence, contents, substance, purport, effect, or meaning of such intercepted communication to any person; and no person not being entitled thereto shall receive or assist in receiving any interstate or foreign communication by wire or radio and use the same or any information therein contained for his own benefit or for the benefit of another not entitled thereto; and no person having received such intercepted communication or having become acquainted with the contents, substance, purport, effect, or meaning of the same or any part thereof, knowing that such information was so obtained, shall divulge or publish the existence, contents, substance, purport, effect, or meaning of the same or any part thereof, or use the same or any information therein contained for his own benefit or for the benefit of another not entitled thereto: *Provided*, that this section shall not apply to the receiving, divulging, publishing, or utilizing the contents of any radio communication broadcast, or transmitted by amateurs or others for the use of the general public, or relating to ships in distress.[256]

Nevertheless, it was essential for purposes of training and the development of improved equipment that intercept work should be undertaken. Even more important was the necessity of having certain fixed stations available in an emergency to undertake the interception of enemy messages. Toward the end of the Fiscal Year 1931, the construction of an experimental intercept station was begun at Battery Cove, Virginia. It was located in the vicinity of Washington, in an area where remotely controlled receivers of radio station WAR served the War Department Message Center in the Munitions Building. Its primary objective was to study the performance of certain recently developed high-speed radio receiving equipment, but it was also to gather actual intercept material for the cryptanalytic practice of personnel of the Signal Intelligence Service.[257]

In the same period also Colonel Joseph O. Mauborgne, then Signal Officer in the Ninth Corps Area, established an unofficial intercept station in the basement of his home in California. He possessed an automatic recording outfit which recorded the intercepted texts on a tape which was then mailed to Washington. Some

---

256. Communications Act of June 19, 1934, Sec. 60-5, 48 Stat. 1103.
257. Supplemental Report to Annual Report, 1931.

intercept activity was also carried on in the Eighth Corps Area, the Panama Canal Department, and the Philippine Department by very small radio intelligence detachments, but these provided the Signal Intelligence Section with only "a fair amount of material for research." Many of these messages were also solved.[258]

Mention should also be made of the establishment in 1933 of a Provisional Radio Intelligence Detachment at Fort Monmouth, First Lieutenant Mark Rhoads, Commanding. While relatively little traffic was intercepted much research and development in the field of radio intelligence was carried on.[259]

By the close of 1937 it was evident that such intercept resources as the United States had developed might shortly be called upon to render actual service in war. In November of that year, it was proposed that a radio intercept station be established in Washington to be used for monitoring the radio channel carrying the bulk of the diplomatic traffic between Washington and New York City, during the twelve of fifteen hours of the day when the most interesting traffic was being handled. The proposal involved the installation of receiving sets at Battery Cove and the War Department Message Center, the installation of the necessary equipment in the Message Center, and the transfer to Washington of two radio operators of suitable qualifications.[260]

The War Plans and Training Division of the Office of the Chief Signal Officer, however, did not concur in the recommendation. The value of the proposed station at Washington was deemed not sufficient to justify the expense which would amount to $5,408.20 initial costs and rental of $72 per month. The Signal Intelligence Section was by this time receiving from other sources more intercept material than it could handle, and had indication of increased activity for which there was insufficient personnel. The establishment of an intercept station at Fort Monmouth was already being contemplated and it was anticipated that it would be able to monitor the circuit suggested for the Washington station. Consequently, it was recommended that the plan for establishing a station at Washington be dropped.[261]

---

258. Major Accomplishments, 1935, par. 10; Supplement to the Annual Report, 1936, sec. 111, par. 5.

259. See *Report on The Provisional Radio Intelligence Detachment for the Period October 1, 1933 to October 17, 1933*, a copy of which is now on file in the Office of the Director of Communications Research, Signal Security Agency. During maneuvers in September 1934, Lieutenant Rhoads served as a signal intelligence unit (there were no others involved) for the Black Side. He succeeded in solving most, if not all, of the messages intercepted. This was the first example of a signal intelligence unit at work in the field since the First World War, as the Provisional Detachment was the first radio intelligence unit to operate since 1918.

260. Memorandum for the Chief Signal Officer from Major W.S. Rumbough, Subject: *Proposal for Establishment of a Radio Intercept Station in Washington*, 19 November 1937, par. 1.

261. *Ibid.*, 4-5.

By 28 February 1938 the Signal Intelligence Service was operating six intercept stations. The installation of the station at Fort Monmouth had been completed. Two other stations were set up within the continental United States; one in the Ninth Corps Area, was located at the Presidio of San Francisco, California, another was established at Fort Sam Houston in the Eighth Corps Area. Authority had been obtained in 1935 for the establishment of signal intelligence detachments at these stations and in overseas departments. As soon as the increase in Signal Corps personnel permitted the organization of such detachments they were established in each of the three overseas departments; one at Quarry Heights in the Panama Canal Department;[262] one at Manila, in the Philippine Department;[263] and one at Fort Shafter, in the Hawaiian Department.[264] The intercepted messages were transmitted to Washington for analysis by registered secret mail in weekly batches.[265]

On 26 January 1938, the Signal Intelligence Detachment at Quarry Heights, Canal Zone, had been directed to attempt 24-hour intercept activity. It was to give first priority to Japanese and Italian diplomatic traffic from Rome to Tokyo, with a secondary emphasis on the same type of traffic transmitted from Berlin to Tokyo. It was also directed to monitor Japanese diplomatic traffic between Tokyo and the Central and South American Countries.[266]

The location of the Signal Intelligence detachments in Hawaii, Panama, and the Eighth and Ninth Corps Areas, however, did not permit the Signal Intelligence Service to take full advantage of the "golden opportunity" to obtain Japanese Army radio traffic presented by the Japanese penetration into China. It was highly desirable that the Japanese Army methods of enciphering and deciphering be studied in order that the code and cipher solution section of the Signal Intelligence Service might have some experience in the analysis of this material. It would prove, of course, of inestimable value in the event of hostilities.[267]

In 1935 the War Department, with the foregoing purpose in view, had established an intercept station at Fort Hughes in the Philippines, with Captain Mark

---

262. Dr. Abraham Sinkov was stationed there as cryptanalyst.

263. This station had no expert cryptanalyst.

264. Dr. S. Kullback was the cryptanalyst here.

265. See Memoranda to each of these Stations from the Chief Signal Officer, 28 February 1938 (SPSIS 320.3); W.F. Friedman to Captain Mark Rhoads, 10 October 1935 (SPSIS 201-Mark Rhoads).

266. Memorandum from the Chief Signal Officer to The Adjutant General, Subject: *Intercept Activity of Signal Intelligence Detachment,* 26 January 1938 (SPSIS 320.3).

267. Chief Signal Officer to The Adjutant General (through G-2), Subject: *Radio Intercept Activity in the Philippine Department,* 9 February 1938 (SPSIS 320.3), par. 1.

Rhoads as officer-in-charge, but he was taken ill a few months thereafter, and was shortly forced to retire from the Army. He was not replaced until March 1938 when Captain Harrod G. Miller, who had graduated from the Signal Intelligence School and afterwards had served as instructor in that school, was sent to the Philippines.

No effective use of officers of similar experience and training had been made in the Philippine Department.   Instead, officers equipped by skill and training for the task had been placed on routine Signal Corps work (e.g. Captain W. Preston Corderman became a Signal Officer, not a Signal Intelligence Officer).   It was requested that a specific directive be issued to the Commanding General, Philippine Department.   Unless the necessary men and equipment were provided for Captain Miller, the effort to activate radio interception through him would prove abortive. Ten enlisted personnel were considered necessary to accomplish the desired monitoring.[268]   The Radio Intelligence Company at Fort Monmouth was also directed to concentrate on Japanese Government traffic from New York to Tokyo, Rome to Tokyo, and Berlin to Tokyo.[269]

By the end of March 1938, the plans for increased intercept activity, which was still prohibited by the Communications Act, required official approval by higher authority in order that it might proceed unimpeded.   It was necessary to protect the War Department and its personnel with a record of official authorization for such activities, applicable, incidentally, to the Navy as well.[270]   A memorandum was therefor transmitted to the Chief of Staff, recommending that authority be granted to the Chief Signal Officer, under the direction of the Assistant Chief of Staff, G-2, "to maintain and operate in time of peace under strictest provisions to insure secrecy, such radio intercept and cryptanalytic services" as were "necessary for training and for national defense purposes."[271]   (The operation of the Signal Intelligence Service had been of value to the Military Intelligence Division.   In two instances it had obtained information which indicated that two foreign powers were "using their diplomatic codes for the transmission of information prejudicial to" American preparations for national defense.)[272]   This recommendation was approved by the Secretary of War, 30 March 1938.[273]

---

268. *Ibid.,* par. 3-4.

269. Chief Signal Officer to Commanding Officer, Fort Monmouth, Subject: *Intercept Directive of Radio Intelligence Company,* 10 February 1938 (SPSIS 320.3).

270. Memorandum for the Chief of Staff from the Assistant Chief of Staff, G-2, 36 March 1938.

271. Memorandum for the Chief of Staff from the Assistant Chief of Staff, G-2, Subject: *Radio Intercepts,* 26 March 1938 (SPSIS 676-3).

272. *Ibid.*

273. *Ibid.,* indorsement by Deputy Chief of Staff.

The intercept activity of the Signal Intelligence Service was consequently accelerated in 1938. On 6 April 1938 the Chief of the Signal Intelligence Service, Major W.O. Reeder,[274] summarized this activity as follows:

> Six months ago only two stations were operating effectively and the mission of these was somewhat general. We are now operating four with good efficiency and one is coming along gradually. The first steps in organizing the work has been to assign channels to each station. Obviously, we cannot cover all the air, and therefore those channels which are currently the most interesting have been assigned. These assignments are not fixed but were made solely as a point of departure. Of course some of these assignments may be found to be beyond the capabilities of certain of the stations. In that event, no greater service can be given by that station than prompt report of its difficulties.[275]

By the end of June 1938, it was evident that the location of the intercept station at Fort Monmouth was unsuitable. It had been operated by the reorganized detachment of the 51st Signal Battalion, the Provisional Radio Intelligence Company. The site, however, was not well-suited for 24-hour radio reception and in addition the occurrence of man-made radio interference made the functioning of the monitoring station difficult. Surveys were made to find a site better adapted to interception and a part of the Fort Hancock, New Jersey, reservation was found to be "vastly superior to any part of Fort Monmouth as a site for a monitoring station."

It was therefore requested that First Lieutenant Earle F. Cook[276] and 18 Signal Corps enlisted men be transferred to Fort Hancock from Fort Monmouth not earlier than 1 September 1938. The station would continue its operation under the direction of the Chief Signal Officer. The estimated cost of this transfer was $2,618.80.[277]

By the autumn of 1938, preparations to send to the overseas departments the necessary cryptographic equipment had been undertaken. It was now possible to supply these units the Converter M-134A which had recently been developed. Meanwhile, the Tenth Signal Company in the Philippines had been strengthened for its prospective intercept activity by the transfer of four radio operators from Fort Monmouth.[278]

---

274. In view of the growth and greatly increasing importance of the activities the Chief Signal Officer deemed it advisable to assign a Regular Army officer as head of the Signal Intelligence Service; Mr. Friedman remained as the principal assistant and chief technical adviser.

275. Memorandum to the Commanding Officer, Provisional Radio Intelligence Company, Fort Monmouth, 6 April 1938 (SPSIS 320.3).

276. First Lieutenant Earle F. Cook, a West Point graduate, rose in rank during World War II. As a Colonel in the Office of the Chief Signal Officer, he was concerned with the activities of the Signal Intelligence Service. From 1945 to 1947 he was Chief of the Army Security Agency in Europe. In 1963 he retired as a Major General. WGB

277. Memorandum to The Adjutant General from the Chief Signal Officer, Subject: *Establishment of Monitoring Station at Fort Hancock, N.J.*, 23 June 1938 (SPSIS 212.2 Fort Monmouth).

278. Third indorsement, The Chief Signal Officer to The Adjutant General 24 June 1938 (SPSIS 320.3).

CRYPTANALYTIC SOLUTIONS

Throughout the period under discussion (1930-1939) attempts were made to solve certain diplomatic traffic within the limits of available staff and facilities, and whenever sufficient volume was available to justify hope of solution. The government which received the greatest attention was, of course, the Japanese. The cryptanalysts of the Signal Intelligence Service had the benefit of the records of solutions made by Yardley's Cipher Bureau in the preceding decade,[279] but not until 1933 was any serious attempt made to resume the attack on Japanese systems. In that year Dr. Kullback and Mr. Hurt were assigned some Japanese encoded messages consisting of two-and-four-letter substitution groups of a Japanese syllabary and small vocabulary. It was not long before they could read them. Although these messages and others provided information of no real value as intelligence, they did provide a basis for a study of the type of vocabulary, the grammatical forms, frequencies, and cryptographic habits to be expected in other Japanese traffic. Typical of the solution activities of this period is that of a system known as "J-6", a three- and four-letter code, which was solved by March 1934.[280]

Between 1933 and 1935 five Japanese diplomatic systems were used in rotation at intervals of three months. These systems, solved and read, were all of the two- and four-letter type of code with syllabary and vocabulary. By 1938 nine Japanese diplomatic systems had been read by the Signal Intelligence Service. The appearance of new systems and the increasing complexity observed in them during the thirties is believed to be the result of the publication in 1931 of Yardley's book, *The American Black Chamber.*[281]

Japanese systems known to the Signal Intelligence Service during the ten years before World War II include the following:

Digraphic substitution	Effective Dates
AW	July 1932 to December 1934
CA	November 1936
YO	September 1938

---

279. See Chapter III.

280. A description of the steps leading to solution is now filed in IR 5010-50-12, together with the traffic and worksheets. The date is 5 March 1934.

281. See *The History of Codes and Ciphers in the United States During the Period Between the World Wars, Part I. 1919-1929*, p. 133 *passim*.

Polygraphic substitution	Effective Dates
XA	1931-1932
XB	?
DA	October 1932 to 15 October 1935
EG	January 1933 to 15 October 1935
WI	April 1933 to October 1934
IK	December 1933 to October 1934
J-6	15 October 1935 to 28 February 1938
J-7	1 January 1936 to 26 February 1936
J-8	1 July 1936 to 31 October 1938
J-9	1 July 1936 to 31 October 1938
J-10	1 November 1938 to 9 April 1939
K-I	1 November 1938
J-11	10 April 1939 to 1 January 1940
KO	April 1939
J-12	2 January 1940 to 31 May 1940
J-13	1 June 1940 to 15 July 1940
J-14	15 July 1940
J-15	15 July 1940
P-I	15 July 1940
J-16	15 August 1940 to 30 November 1940

The Japanese introduced transposition as an encipherment of various codes. Usually the transpositions had to be designated in the traffic by an indicator. The following systems were known: ALYTA, ETOME, FIPUF, one without indicator, YMMBO, XUMFO, POSTA, BYWDE, VOSAI, KALNY, VERDI. Transposition was applied to the various codes as follows:

Code	Effective Dates
XA	1931
K-1	19 January 1939 to 1 July 1940
K-2	19 January 1939
K-3	1 July 1940

Code	Effective Dates
K-4	15 July 1940 to 15 November 1940
K-5	15 August 1940 to 30 November 1940
K-6	1 December 1940 to 28 February 1941
K-7	
K-8	1 March 1941
K-9	11 March to 25 April 1941
K-10	23 June 1941 to 15 August 1943

The following spelling tables were also used:

JE English Spelling

English Spelling and Vocabulary

French Spelling and Vocabulary

HE Code

EX Code

OG Code

UJ Code

CH Code

B Table

PA English Spelling

CA English Spelling

In the early days of the Signal Intelligence Service furnishing the translations of foreign texts was not expected by G-2. When translations were made, they were for some time not forwarded to G-2 at all but were kept within the Signal Intelligence Service, Beginning in January 1935 the translations of certain messages were occasionally shown to the Chief Signal Officer. Soon there came a change in policy and in April 1936 the *Bulletin* was established as a proper means of bringing to the attention of G-2 and the War Department the texts of solved messages deemed to be of importance.

Japanese diplomatic traffic supplied the first translations for the *Bulletin*. The personnel employed in this early solution work, under the general supervision of Mr. Friedman, were Rowlett, Kullback, and Sinkov, and later Ferner, Snyder, Clark, and Bearce. By 1938 Mr. Rowlett had the direct supervision of Japanese solutions; and very importantly he and Mr. Ferner concentrated in particular on breaking the Japanese machine cipher, known to the Signal Intelligence Service as the "Red System."[282]

Though the Signal Intelligence Service had already studied a number of cipher machines during tests, the first study of a machine cipher in actual use by a foreign government was the Japanese Red machine. As the machine was first known, it contained two wheels, one to encipher the six vowels and the other to encipher the twenty consonants separately. Thus the resulting cipher text was composed of vowels enciphered only by vowels and consonants enciphered only by consonants—an attempt to reduce telegraphic expense by producing artificial words in the cipher text. Later the "six" wheel was used for any six letters. A third wheel controlled the motion of the cipher wheels. In addition to the daily cipher sequences, 240 indicators for the wheel settings had to be solved. The system, put into use before 1932, was undertaken for study in 1935 and solved by 1936. On 1 December 1938 the machine was modified by the addition of three special commutators of interrupted motion to encipher highly secret messages. The last message received in this system was dated 21 August 1941. It was superseded by the more secure and today well-publicized "Purple Machine."

The friendly rivalry which had existed between the Signal Intelligence Service and the Code and Signal Section of the Navy in the solution of test messages was also evident in the task of interception and subsequent solution of diplomatic traffic. Each services attempted to intercept as much material as possible, to solve it immediately, and to gain credit for itself as the agency by which the information obtained was made available to the Government. Such a condition was, of course, highly undesirable, and steps were taken to eliminate the feeling of rivalry as much as possible. The first steps were, however, anything but successful. It was agreed after lengthy negotiations that the Army and the Navy would exchange all diplomatic traffic from their intercept facilities, and that both services would work on this traffic. But in order to avoid as much duplication of effort as possible it was agreed that the Army would be responsible for the solution of all traffic of days with an even date and the Navy all traffic of days with an odd date. This arrangement was deemed by the Chief Signal Officer and the Director of Naval Communications to be the most practical one, since all available traffic was necessary for solution and it was desirable to give both services equal opportunities for training, "credit," and so on.

---

282. At this period colors were used as short titles; though they have been officially abandoned except for subordinate phases of systems, this short title is still used colloquially.

ANALOG OF JAPANESE CIPHER MACHINE KNOWN AS PURPLE MACHINE

These early electric typewriters with ciphering mechanism between them duplicated the Japanese diplomatic cipher machine Angoo Kikai Taipu B, known to Allied cryptanalysts as the Purple Machine.

PART OF ORIGINAL JAPANESE "PURPLE MACHINE"

Part of the Japanese cipher machine Angoo Kikai Taipu B, found at the conclusion of the war in Europe in a building occupied by the Japanese embassy staff. Known to Allied cryptanalysts as the Purple Machine, this and three similar items discovered with it were the only parts of the original Japanese cipher machine ever recovered. Note that the cipher machine used stepping relays, usually used in telephone switching systems, instead of rotors.

CRYPTANALYSIS IN THE DEPARTMENTS[283]

One of the plans made for the Signal Intelligence Service in 1930 had included the sending of civilian cryptanalysts to work in Panama, Hawaii, and the Philippines, but no steps were taken to carry out this recommendation until it was learned in 1936[284] that G-2 in Panama was employing an amateur cryptanalyst and "thereby infringing upon the prerogatives of the Chief Signal Officer."[285] The civilian chief of the Signal Intelligence Service therefore recommended that if a cryptanalytic unit was thought to be essential at that time in the Panama Department, one of his assistants should be sent there to establish such a unit under the Signal Officer. Although the staff in Washington was small, this arrangement would not result in "losing the services of a man ... but merely having him do in the field much of the work he now does, with the results immediately available to those who want them in Panama." He believed that the inevitable slowing of the work would have less serious consequences than the decentralization of signal intelligence activities which would result from the taking over of cryptanalytic functions by G-2, and hoped that the plan would result in obtaining backing from the Department Commanders for the work of the Signal Intelligence Service.[286]

To implement these recommendations in July 1936[287] Dr. Sinkov was sent to Panama where he reported to the Department Commander for duty. No written instructions had been given him in Washington and contact with him during his stay in Panama was maintained partly through channels and partly through personal correspondence.[288]

An intercept station was set up in Panama during Dr. Sinkov's stay[289] and apparently its program was influenced to some extent by the needs of the Signal Intelligence Service in Washington. Intercepts of Japanese messages were forwarded to Washington; those of other governments were classified and kept on file in Panama.[290] Dr. Friedman wrote in the summer of 1937:

---

283. The three departments were in the Panama Canal Zone, Hawaii, and the Philippines. WGB

284. Memorandum for Major Rumbough, signed W.F. Friedman, 16 January 1936 (SPSIS 201: A. Sinkov). The sources of all statements in this section are the 201 files of A. Sinkov (Panama Department) and S. Kullback (Hawaii Department).

285. Major W.O. Reeder, *Duties of Civilian Cryptanalysts in Hawaii and Panama*, 15 October 1937.

286. W.F. Friedman, Memo for Major Rumbough, 16 January 1936.

287. Letter of A. Sinkov to his friends in the SIS, dated 2 October 1936, in which he says that he left Washington three months earlier.

288. Memorandum cited in footnote 287.

289. Sinkov to Friedman, 16 April 1937: "The radio equipment for the intercept station will arrive on the next boat and I am hopeful that we will be able to begin our intercept program by the first of the next month."

290. Sinkov to Friedman, 30 June and 15 July 1937; Friedman to Sinkov, 26 July 1937.

> I would ... very much appreciate your sending on all J intercept material.   Our station at Fort Monmouth has gone to pot since they took all the men away for the Texas exercise. As a result, we are getting very little European material and if you could get any of that for us, it would be appreciated.[291]

While in Panama Dr. Sinkov continued to work on Japanese Governmental systems.   He was given material for the solution of diplomatic codes and ciphers and was taught the solution of the Red Cipher Machine[292] which had been solved in Washington about this time, in order that he might work on the current diplomatic system, "submitting occasional translations to G-2."[293]   He was, however, handicapped by lack of material.[294]   In the summer of 1937 the decision was made to discontinue work in the field on Japanese systems.

The director wrote:

> I think you can deduce the reasons when I tell you that they are based entirely on the desirability of avoiding the demise of the proverbial goose.[295]

Obviously, it was thought that activity in the Department might prove a danger to the security of cryptanalytic operations.

The decision placed Dr. Sinkov in a difficult position.   The Signal Officer in the Department was in the habit of submitting some of the diplomatic messages to the Commanding General in order to win support for the intercept activity.   If no more Japanese messages were to be read and translated, it would prove difficult to maintain this support.   A compromise was therefore evolved.   While work on the diplomatic traffic ceased, Dr. Sinkov continued to produce for the Signal Officer translations of messages in the simple commercial system — the Department even provided an officer who had been a language student in Japan to aid in production.[296]

During the remainder of his stay in Panama Dr. Sinkov gave some time to the study of Italian Government messages.   They were chosen because, of the European "Axis" stations, interception was easier in the case of Italy.[297]

Meanwhile, in March 1937[298] Dr. Solomon Kullback was sent to Hawaii,

---

291. Friedman to Sinkov, 2 August 1937.

292. Memorandum cited in note 284.

293. Sinkov to Friedman, 16 April 1937.

294. Sinkov to Friedman, 15 July 1937.

295. Friedman to Sinkov, 2 August 1937; 1 September 1937.

296. Sinkov to Friedman, 12 September and 15 November 1937.

297. Sinkov to Friedman, 19 August 1937.

298. Major W.S. Rumbough to Commanding General, Hawaiian Department, 15 February 1937.

ABRAHAM SINKOV

Colonel Abraham Sinkov, one of William F. Friedman's principal assistants, was Commanding Officer, Central Bureau, Brisbane, Australia, from 1942 to 1945. In the Pacific Theater of Operations, he was largely responsible for leading the U.S. Army's efforts to break the Japanese code systems. In 1946 he was appointed Chief, Security Division, Army Security Agency, and later he headed a major office of the National Security Agency. After retirement in 1962 he and his wife, also a former employee of the Signal Intelligence Service, moved to Phoenix where for some years he taught courses in computer science and cryptography at Arizona State University.

SOLOMON KULLBACK

Colonel Solomon Kullback, a renowned mathematician and statistician, was one of William F. Friedman's principal assistants. He was Chief, Military Cryptanalytic Branch, Signal Security Agency, from 1942 to 1945, when he became Chief, Research and Development Division, Army Security Agency. In June, 1946 he reverted to inactive duty. Today Dr. Kullback is a Professor Emeritus at George Washington University, Washington, D.C.

apparently in response to a request for a code clerk.[299]   He received no written instructions in Washington but reported for duty to be assigned by the Commanding General of the Hawaii Department.[300]

The cryptographic duties did not occupy much time.   Soon after his arrival Dr. Kullback reported that "except when messages may pile up unduly, I will not be called on to do *all* the encoding, etc., of War department traffic.[301]   No other mention of this task appears in the correspondence except one reference to the effect that arrangements were being made to have the work done by others.[302]

Dr. Kullback's most valuable work during his brief stay in Hawaii was in obtaining interesting intercept material for the Signal Intelligence Service in Washington.[303]   He helped to reconstruct the Japanese diplomatic net and what was believed to be a kana military net in which several Navy stations were found, [304] and was obviously able to give expert advice on the traffic which should have priority.[305] By September, however, he evidently thought that he had accomplished all that could be done along these lines because he wrote:

> From my experience to date I would say that it were better for somebody from the office (in Washington) to visit these stations, say yearly, or once every two years, to maintain closer and personal contact, than to assign a cryptanalyst.[306]

At the time of Dr. Kullback's departure for Hawaii it had been intended that he continue work on the solution of Japanese diplomatic codes and ciphers with material from Washington[307] but before the necessary charts and tables were sent, the loyalty of one of the enlisted men in the intelligence detachment at Honolulu came under suspicion, [308] and the material was never sent.   Dr. Kullback was

---

299. Major W.O. Reeder, *Duties of Civilian Cryptanalysts in Hawaii and Panama,* 15 October 1937: "...if he (Kullback) was not sent in response to this request, the coincidence was chronological at least." It should be pointed out that while Dr. Kullback was competent to serve as a code clerk, he was much more expert than was necessary for such a position.

300. *Ibid.*

301. Kullback to Friedman, 25 March 1937.

302. Kullback to Friedman, 6 April 1937.

303. Friedman to Kullback, 24 June 1937; 2 August 1937.

304. Kullback to Friedman, 6 April 1937, 27 May 1937, 17 September 1937.

305. Kullback to Friedman, 16 July 1937.

306. Kullback to Friedman, 17 September 1937.

307. Major W.O. Reeder, Duties of Civilian Cryptanalysts in Hawaii and Panama, 15 October 1937.

308. *Ibid.*; Friedman to Kullback, 14 April 1937.

advised not to attempt to reconstruct the tables,[309] He did some work, however, on Japanese diplomatic and Rikugun systems[310] and other material was sent him from Washington.[311] He reported that he had never used enlisted men on this project and "kept all idea of the J systems from them"[312]

While in Hawaii Dr. Kullback began a study of German systems, concentrating on a four-letter code with the help of an enlisted man who knew German.[313] He also revised for publication his paper on Statistical Methods[314] and worked on solution of the Kryha Cipher Machine.[315]

His relations with G-2 in the Department presented no difficulties. They were apparently satisfied with translations of plain-text Rikugun messages the content of which might later be found in *The New York Times*.[316]

The decision to recall both cryptanalysts to Washington was made because of the very greatly increased burden of the work being done by the SIS in Washington and because it was believed that their services could be put to better use in Washington than in isolation in a Department.[317] The cryptanalysts themselves were in agreement with this decision. Dr. Kullback wrote on 17 September 1937:

> I think that I can be of much more service in Washington than here ...
> We have neither the facilities nor the assistance to carry out real
> solution activities here and in any case the results of the same are of
> interest to Washington, not here ...

309. Captain Harrod G. Miller to Kullback, 17 May 1937.

310. Japanese Army systems. WGB

311. Kullback to Friedman, 23 April 1937; Friedman to Kullback, 7 May 1937; Kullback to Friedman, June 1937; Friedman to Kullback, 24 June 1937.

312. Kullback to Friedman, 17 September 1937, but see letter in which he speaks of working with one of the enlisted men and says "... if you feel that you can lend us ... some of the Rikugun messages we could make copies of them here and send the originals back to you." Kullback to Friedman June 1937. Friedman replied, "I have gotten together ... the Rikugun stuff and will send them on." Friedman to Kullback, 24 June 1937.

313. Kullback to Friedman, June 1937; 16 July 1937.

314. Friedman to Kullback, 27 November 1937; Kullback to Friedman, 3 February 1938; Friedman to Kullback, 14 February 1938.

315. Friedman to Kullback, 24 June 1937.

316. Kullback to Friedman, 17 September 1937.

317. Friedman to Kullback, 1 September 1937; Friedman to Sinkov, same date. Major W.O. Reeder, *Duties of the Civilian Cryptanalysts in Hawaii and Panama*, 15 October 1937.

SECRET INKS

The specialized nature of the responsibilities of the Signal Intelligence Service in connection with secret inks also demanded highly qualified, technically trained personnel. At the close of the Fiscal Year 1931, steps were taken to establish a laboratory for research in the field of invisible inks and to obtain the necessary equipment and supplies within the limits of the small funds available. Originally it had been contemplated that this work would be conducted at Fort Monmouth but the establishment of a laboratory more conveniently located for War Department work was desirable.[318]

It was proposed that secret ink investigations be undertaken as soon as qualified personnel could be obtained. In 1931 this work was performed by a Military Intelligence Reserve Officer, Captain A.J. McGrail, who was considered the leading American expert in the field of secret inks. The Chief Signal Officer, then Major General Irving J. Carr, recommended that the enforced dependence on an officer outside the Signal Corps for such investigations be remedied as soon as possible. He requested that funds be made available by the Fiscal Year 1934 for the employment of a secret ink chemist, who possessed special training along these lines.[319]

In 1932 Captain McGrail was transferred to the Signal Corps Reserve. He was ordered to active duty with the Signal Intelligence Service for the customary two-week periods. During these terms of active service he worked in the small laboratory and "was able to impart some valuable information relative to methods and processes of detecting secret-ink writing" to two selected members of the Signal Intelligence Service.[320]

This method of instruction was continued until regularly employed personnel could make the tests of a routine character, but Captain McGrail was still consulted in the more difficult cases. It was therefore considered expedient to employ a chemist with specialized training, if he could be found, as soon as funds permitted.[321] The personnel authorized for the entire service, however, remained static and the slight increase authorized toward the end of the decade was diverted to more urgent tasks.

---

318. Supplemental Report to the Annual Report, 1931, p. 2d.

319. *Ibid.*

320. Annual Report, 1932, p. 8.

321. *Ibid.*

CAPTAIN LAURENCE F. SAFFORD

Captain Laurence F. Safford, U.S. Navy, was one of the first U.S. Naval Officers to specialize in cryptography and cryptanalysis. He is perhaps most known for his development of the Navy's ECM, known to the Army as the M-138-C or SIGABA. He was Special Assistant to the Director, Armed Forces Security Agency, from 1949 to 1951. In 1958 Congress awarded him $100,000 for his wartime contributions.

CHAPTER IV

IN RETROSPECT

The reader has already noted that, except for occasional digressions in which the events of World War II have been anticipated in order to show more clearly the significance of earlier developments, the narrative of the preceding chapters, which cover the same period, has in general been ended with the year 1939. The reason is, of course, obvious: prior to 1939 the activity of the Signal Intelligence Service had consisted generally of preparation for a hypothetical war, though, to be sure, there was a strong emphasis upon a war with Japan motivated by Japan's operations on the Asiatic mainland and the precarious state of Japanese-American relations since World War I. After the beginning of 1939, however, events in Europe made it increasingly clear that in that quarter lay an equal, if not, indeed, a greater, danger to the peace of the United States.

Though for the twenty-seven months between the attack on Poland (1 September 1939) and that on Pearl Harbor (7 December 1941) the Signal Intelligence Service was still in a sense engaged in preparation for war rather than in actual conflict, henceforth that activity had indeed entered a new and greatly accelerated phase. For this reason, the the present text is in a sense a prolegomenon of the history of codes and ciphers during World War II, a text which must await the future to be published.

Before concluding this text, however, it might be well to summarize the achievements of the Signal Intelligence Service in the nearly ten years after its founding in 1930. This can best be done by a comparison of the situation which existed in 1939 with that which existed prior to the mobilization of 1917. It will be recalled[322] that in 1917 the United States Army was faced with the responsibility of both protecting its own communications and that of attacking the communications of potential enemies.[323]

---

322. See *History of Codes and Ciphers in the United States During World War I.*

323. While unpreparedness in the fields of traffic analysis and cryptanalysis, two important means of attacking the communications of potential enemies, was probably no greater in 1917 than in other phases of military science, it should be said in defense of the U.S. Army that in these early years the art of radio communications was only beginning to undergo large-scale development. Indeed, World War I was the first in which radio communications played a significant part.

The Chief Signal Officer had, indeed, been officially entrusted with the task of code compilation but the only code ready for use was a one-part affair, provided with a not very secure form of encipherment for the more secret messages, and it had been printed under insecure conditions and was believed, with, as it proved, complete justification, to be already compromised. No unit within the Army was charged with solution. Indeed, there were only three officers who were regarded as expert in the field. Thus it was that reliance had to be placed at least for a time on the efforts of the cryptanalysts at Riverbank Laboratories.[324] Both in Washington and in France, the Army was forced to build new organizations from the very beginning and this while the War was already in progress. What is surprising is that anything was achieved in the eighteen months during which the War lasted. In fact, personnel engaged in the work were hardly seasoned before the Armistice rendered their efforts largely no longer necessary.

In comparison with this state of unpreparedness in 1917, the Army approached the outbreak of what proved to be World War II reasonably well prepared. In spite of the extremely limited funds available for the entire signal-intelligence program, much was accomplished. A group of Regular Army officers had been trained in all phases of signal intelligence and were ready for administrative duties on high levels. A nucleus of expert cryptanalysts, while far from adequate in number to face the tasks which ultimately they were assigned, had been thoroughly trained in all methods of solution then known. The art of cryptanalysis had been developed along scientific lines far beyond the highest point of efficiency reached in World War I and the groundwork was well laid for still greater advances when, in actual operations, new problems would present the necessity for finding new solutions. Automatic machinery had been placed in the service of statistical analysis to make possible computations not hitherto dreamed of. Cryptanalytic continuity, which had been broken off completely in 1930 at the time of the dissolution of the Cipher Bureau, had, at least in the case of the Japanese systems, been resumed. Intercept stations had been established for the systematic gathering of the raw material without which there is no hope of cryptanalytic solution. The chief deficiency in the field of solution was the fact that lack of funds prevented the training of enough cryptanalysts.

For the protection of Army communications, an ambitious program of code compilation had been completed, made possible by the then revolutionary use of tabulating machinery. Moreover, the manual ciphers had been greatly perfected and were far more secure than the best that had been used by the Army in World War I, yet even more significant advances in this field were made in the development of automatic cryptographic machinery. Early versions of the M-134 cipher machines had been put into production and were in some cases in use. A more valuable

---

324. That Herbert O. Yardley, who founded the Cipher Bureau, MI-8, in June 1917, and who was commissioned as a first lieutenant, Signal Corps Reserve, on 29 June 1917, should largely be ignored by the writers of this history at this point in time can perhaps be understood in view of their unsympathetic feeling for him. In this connection, see *The History of Codes and Ciphers in the United States During World War I,* Chapter I. WGB

machine, the M-134-C (SIGABA), with even greater security, had been invented — though later phases of its development had been carried on the by Navy, the basic ideas underlying the machine were contributed by personnel of the Signal Intelligence Service — and was, though the Army did not know it in 1939, almost ready for production. These machines subsequently served as the basis for all research and development in World War II in the field of automatic cryptographic machinery. Though limited funds prevented any real development of methods for the protection of speech communications and picture communications, these had been at least conceived. A small beginning, also, had made for the provision of secret ink facilities, though here again lack of money prevented the development which was known to be desirable.

Thus it will be seen that the Signal Intelligence Service, while in no way failing to exploit the experience of World War I in the field of cryptology, had never blindly assumed that if and when another conflict broke out, it would be merely a repetition of the same conditions as had been encountered in 1917-1918. Careful attention had been paid to all of the scientific research and development which had made possible the use of new, speedier, and more secure techniques of signal communications.

The Signal Intelligence Service was therefore well prepared for the task which faced it. Looking backward over the whole period of the peace, it is possible now to see that the two chief problems which in those years hampered progress were one, the lack of unified control over all phases of cryptology during the first decade, and two, the extremely limited funds with which the Signal Intelligence Service had to do all that was necessary in the second.

INDEX